D0272201

A NEW ROMANTIC
ANTHOLOGY

A
NEW ROMANTIC
ANTHOLOGY

edited by
STEFAN SCHIMANSKI
and
HENRY TREECE

London
THE GREY WALLS PRESS LTD
Crown Passage, Pall Mall

*First published in 1949
by the Grey Walls Press Limited
7 Crown Passage, Pall Mall, London, S.W.1
Printed in Great Britain
by Western Printing Services Limited
Bristol*

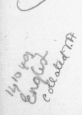

CONTENTS

GENERAL ESSAYS
ON ROMANTICISM AND APOCALYPSE

PARTICULAR ESSAYS
ON ROMANTICISM IN MODERN POETRY,
THE CINEMA AND THE NOVEL

ROMANTICISM IN POETRY

ANTHOLOGIES OF CONTEMPORARY WRITING
ENGLISH POETRY
Selected and introduced by Alex Comfort

CONTENTS

IRISH POETRY

Selected and introduced by Patrick MacDonogh

SCOTTISH POETRY

Selected and introduced by Maurice Lindsay

CONTENTS

WELSH POETRY
Selected and introduced by Glyn Jones

ROMANTICISM IN THE SHORT STORY
Selected and introduced by Peter Goffin

ACKNOWLEDGEMENTS

THE General Editors, Stefan Schimanski and Henry Treece, wish it to be understood that this anthology is in no way intended as the expression of any particular Group or Movement. It is neither Apocalyptic nor Personalist; but it is an attempt to show how widely spread is the Romantic attitude in British writing today.

Furthermore, in their Introduction, the General Editors are putting forward their own personal views, which are not necessarily those of any of the contributors.

The sections devoted to poetry and to stories were chosen and edited independently and entirely by their respective editors, Alex Comfort, Patrick MacDonogh, Maurice Lindsay, Glyn Jones and Peter Goffin, to whom is due all credit no less than responsibility.

The poetry sections are placed in the conventional order of England, Ireland, Scotland and Wales. No criticism is implied by their relative positions in this book.

The General Editors wish to express their added thanks to Alex Comfort, Maurice Lindsay and Patrick MacDonogh, who have allowed their own work to be published in the poetry sections; to Herbert Read for allowing them to piece together certain extracts from his work on Romanticism; and to Mervyn Peake for so readily making available the drawings which he made when writing *Titus Groan*.

Acknowledgements for permission to reprint work in this book are due to Mr. Herbert Read and Faber & Faber Ltd. for 'To a Conscript of 1940', from *A World within a War*, and extracts from *Annals of Innocence and Experience*, *Collected Essays*, and *Surrealism*; Mr. Alex Comfort and George Routledge & Sons Ltd. for 'Eighth Elegy', from *Elegies*, and *Life and Letters Today* for 'An Exposition of Irresponsibility'; Mr. Ainslie Ellis and *Poetry Folios* for 'Supreme Anarchy'; Mr. John Heath-Stubbs and *Poetry Folios* for 'The Dancing Floor of Britomartis'; Mr. Os Marron and *Poetry Folios* for 'From the North-Country';

ACKNOWLEDGEMENTS

Mr. Paul Potts and *Poetry Folios* for 'No', 'A Poet's Testament', 'A Ballad for Britons'; Mr. Stephen Spender and *Poetry Folios* for 'A Conscript'; Mr. Peter Ure and *Poetry Folios* for 'The Winter Palace' and 'In the City'; Mr. Nicholas Moore and *Poetry Folios* for 'The Hairsbreadth', and the Fortune Press for 'Charley didn't have a New Master' and 'Prayer to Nobody'; Mr. J. F. Hendry and *Life and Letters Today* for 'The Ship'; Mr. Adam Drinan and *Maryland Quarterly* for 'Successful Scot'; Mrs. Alun Lewis and George Allen & Unwin Ltd. for 'In Hospital', from *Ha! Ha! Among the Trumpets*; Mr. Roland Mathias and George Routledge & Sons Ltd. for 'The Bearers', from *Break in Harvest*; Mr. Huw Menai and Chapman & Hall Ltd. for 'Autumn' from *The Simple Vision*; Mr. Keidrych Rhys for 'Alarm, Alarm'; Mr. Dylan Thomas and the Parton Bookshop for 'Light Breaks where no Sun Shines', from *Eighteen Poems*; Mr. Vernon Watkins and Faber & Faber Ltd. for 'Griefs of the Sea', from *The Ballad of the* Mari Llwyd; Mr. Idris Davies and Faber & Faber Ltd. for 'One February Night', from *Tonypandy*; Mr. George Ewart Evans for 'The Pursuit'; Mr. David Jones and Faber & Faber Ltd. for the section from 'In Parenthesis'; Mr. Wyn Griffith and *The Welsh Review* for sections from 'The Barren Tree'; Mr. Austin Clarke and *The Dublin Magazine* for 'The Lucky Coin'; Mr. Padraic Fallon and *The Dublin Magazine* for the section from 'Raftery's Dispute with the Whiskey'; Mr. Donagh MacDonagh and *The Dublin Magazine* for 'Migrant'; Mr. Patrick MacDonogh and *The Dublin Magazine* for 'The Widow of Drynam'; Mr. Roy McFadden and *The Dublin Magazine* for 'Elegy'; Mr. Valentin Iremonger and *The Irish Times* for 'Poem'; Mr. Seumas O'Sullivan and *The Irish Times* for '1939'; Mr. John Hewitt and *The Bell* for 'The Glens'; Mr. Bruce Williamson and *The Bell* for 'Poem'; acknowledgements are also due in respect of the following publications: 'The Lucky Coin' (*Night and Morning*, the Orwell Press); 'Pastorale' by Mr. J. Lyle Donaghy (*Wilderness Sings*, Author); 'The Ecstasy of Colmcille' by Mr. Robert Farren (*The First Exile*, Sheed & Ward); 'This Alien World' by Mr. Robert Greacen (*One Recent Evening*, the Favil Press); 'The Glens' (*Irish Poems of Today*); 'Poem' by Mr. Valentin Iremonger (*Poems from Ireland*); 'The Soldiers' by Mr. John Irvine (*Willow Leaves*,

ACKNOWLEDGEMENTS

the Talbot Press); 'The Great Hunger' by Mr. Patrick Kavanagh (*The Great Hunger*, the Cuala Press); 'The Widow of Drynam' (*Over the Water*, the Orwell Press, *Editor's Choice, The Best Poems of 1943*); 'Elegy' (*Flowers for a Lady*, Routledge); '1939' (*The Collected Poems of Seumas O'Sullivan*, the Orwell Press, *Poems from Ireland*); 'Poem' by Mr. Bruce Williamson (*On the Barricades*, New Frontiers Press); and a general acknowledgement is also due, together with an apology, to all authors or publishers we may have overlooked. Finally, our grateful thanks for the readiness with which both poets and publishers granted their permission for selected works to be used in this book, and our sincere apologies to those writers whose work has unavoidably been omitted owing to limitations of space.

S. K. S.
H. T.

GENERAL ESSAYS
ON
ROMANTICISM AND APOCALYPSE

INTRODUCTION
The Personalist View of Romanticism

IF Romanticism is an arabesque, Classicism is a pair of parallel lines, meeting nowhere, or at infinity, which is even beyond death. If Classicism is sunlight, Romanticism is black midnight and the Northern Lights hanging their coloured curtains in the sky. If Classicism is science, knowledge, defined and definite, Romanticism is that fantasy and speculation which allows man a brief glimpse of his godhead.

If the artist is a sick man, then the Romantic artist alleviates this sickness and fills the gaps in his personality by creating a plenitude of experience, for himself and for others, by the use of his maker's fantasy. The Classicist, on the other hand, ignores the wide horizons of the imagination and restricts his vision to the confines of a limited manner.

The Classicist has his style made ready for him, at his hand, whatever the value of his statement, a mechanical formula, originated centuries ago and remaining static and oblivious of man's new explorations and discoveries. The Realist endeavours, as Herbert Read says in *Politics of the Unpolitical,* 'to give an exact representation of the external world', shows this world as a camera would, untransmuted by the strength and the subtleties of the personality. But the Romantic must discover, out of suffering and despair, his own style and approach, must because of his divine spirit display his individual vision, that hallmark of the unique personality.

Which is to say that Classicism selects, ignoring that which might ruin its formal design (Baroque apart, which is the introduction into a formal pattern of a fantastic element). Realism presents all that is seen with the physical eye, ignoring man's nature as a spiritual being. But Romanticism transforms what is seen by the majesty of the personality, and calls on all the resources, colour, music, rhythmic variety, of the artistic spirit to produce a *whole* world in which the imaginative man may move freely.

The Classicist and the Realist work with the head on the head; the Romantic on the heart. The Classicist is occupied with *things in their unity*; the Romantic with *men in their diversity*. For the Romantic is as young in his spirit as the Classicist is staid and set in his habits; Classicism admits no development, but Romanticism working at the core of chaos creates for itself a fervent desire to embrace nothing less than the whole world, sees tears as well as laughter, corruption as well as health, and death as well as life.

The Romantic is unafraid. He must meet fear so that he may tear off its mask and find compassion. Whatever is concealed must be made apparent, if man's mind is to achieve balance. All hidden things are fearful and produce a curious horror in the observer (see Henry Moore's 'Crowd of People looking at a tied-up Object', *Transformation One*). The medieval craftsmen, true Romantics in their terrifying externalizations of the individual personality and concept, brought their spiritual fears into the daylight in the shape of horrifying gargoyles. To expose a terror is to conquer it.

The Romantic artist strives towards new equations in the illumination of his subject; and each equation is a subjective one, something quite new, growing out of the persona of the author, yet striking an immediate and sympathetic chord in the reader, for whom, hereafter, the original object of description will be enriched.

For the Romantic artist is the advance-guard of human sensibility, who leaves the artistic world (and the ordinary world, as evidence the influence of Ben Nicholson and Mac-Knight Kauffer on railway advertisements) richer than he found it.

Such an artist searches for a completion, a pattern and a purpose in the tumultuous world about him. He looks for a new relationship of things to replace an outdated tiredness and a debility and depression of description. He uses his creative personality to bring about such a pattern and such a relationship.

Surrealism is Romantic in *concept*, but often, as in Chirico's landscapes, is Classical in *execution*. Yet it fails as an artistic philosophy since it either only states an *attitude* or at other times stretches the boundaries of fantasy to the point at which no message is apparent or comprehensible.

And all art must have a message, must indicate a way of life.

Apocalypticism expressed faith in man's freedom, wholeness, and necessity for organic living; and disagreed with the common lack of humanity shown by most political systems. It stated, among other things,

That man was in need of greater freedom, economic no less than aesthetic, from machines and from mechanistic living.

That no existent political system, Left or Right; no artistic ideology, Surrealism or the political school of Auden, was able to provide this freedom.

That the Machine Age had exerted too strong an influence on art.

That Myth, as a means of integrating the personality within Society, had been neglected and despised.

Man's freedom can only come to him from within, for he alone can discover his vocation and be its final judge; no one else, no individual, no collective group can take away this duty and fight his personal battles in his personal world. This is the mainspring of Herbert Read's concept of Anarchism.

Social responsibility is one of the essentials of Personalism, which, to quote Emmanuel Mounier, has 'the simplicity and disinterestedness of men who truly serve man'; Personalism aims at a balance, at a unity between the person and the social group, and strives for the integration of freedom with co-operation. It believes that no creative spirit can exist without the freedom of choice, but that without co-operation that creative spirit becomes so selfish and ingrown that it ultimately destroys itself.

Man was born free and must be given the means to find his

freedom. This freedom is his right to choose—even to choose wrong if he shall ever learn to choose right. Truth is not a statement of fact, or a straight line, or a mathematical equation. It is a condition—the condition of grace—and it is born out of its own contradiction.

One may only find truth by exploration, by failures and successes, by suffering and joy. It shows itself in paradoxes and extremes. So, to discover it, the Romantic mind allows its images to fly freely, sometimes as vast as the landscape of Gormenghast, sometimes as minute as a point of light in the humming-bird's small eye. But the Classical mind, or what we would call the staid and restricted personality, for whom life's adventure has ceased, has no time, no necessity, and no energy for such a freedom of search. It requires rather that the whole world should be as formal, as precise, as immediately comprehensible—and as sterile—as a Georgian garden. It is afraid of the very element which makes man capable of greatness, the personality.

If Classicism is the mask, Realism is the face behind that mask. But Romanticism is the soaring spirit, that spark of the Creator, which will flash one day out of the tired eyes, to glimpse and enjoy the paradise that God intended.

S. S. and H. T.

HERBERT READ

ON ROMANTICISM

MANY writers, especially novelists, have written in accordance with some theory of the nature of personality, and an inquiry into such working theories would be of great interest. But that is an aspect of the subject which I should like to exclude from the present inquiry, which is to be concerned not so much with personality, as objectively conceived by the writer, as with the writer's own personality—the subjective nature of personality, the part it plays in the process of writing: what, briefly, we might call the creative function of the personality. This is, perhaps, a vague subject, but its very vagueness is the excuse I offer for dealing with it. If we can introduce a few definitions into this twilight, a good service to criticism will have been rendered. As it is at present, this word 'personality' is tossed about, a more or less meaningless counter, from critic to critic. There is scarcely a literary judgement made anywhere in recent times that does not resolve itself into a statement such as: 'The work of so and so is good because it is the perfect expression of his personality.'

We cannot hope to arrive at a definition of personality without encroaching to some extent on the science of psychology.

I believe that criticism must concern itself, not only with the work of art itself, but also with the process of writing, and with the writer's state of mind when inspired—that is to say, criticism must concern itself, not only with the finished work of art, but also with the workman, his mental activity and his tools.

If we depart a single pace from the consideration of the work of art in isolation from all personal questions we involve ourselves in psychological considerations. It might be possible, for example, to plunge into the quarrel of Romantics and Classics with nothing in our armoury but an objective measuring-rod. An infallible distinction might be found in the use of the letter *p* in feminine rhymes and false quantities; it would be infallible, but it would be dull. We should separate the sheep and goats, but the really interesting question—why some people are goats, and others sheep—that question would be left unsolved.

Freud says that 'in every individual there is a coherent organization of mental processes which we call his *ego*'; and this may serve as the *preliminary* definition of personality of which I am in search. This ego is identical with the conscious flow of our thoughts, the impressions we receive, the sensations we experience. Also, from this ego, this *coherent organization* of mental processes, according to Freud, proceed the repressions 'by means of which an attempt is made to cut off certain trends in the mind not merely from consciousness, but also from their other forms of manifestation and activity'. Freud, following another Austrian writer, Georg Groddeck, further claims that the conduct of the ego throughout life is essentially passive—we are 'lived', as it were, by unknown and uncontrollable forces. But presumably these forces are inherent, differentiated in each individual—being, in fact, that reserve of instincts and passions which normally we repress, but which are never securely under the control of our conscious reason. To this reserve Freud gives the name Id, for it is the impersonal aspect of the Ego.

Near to the word 'personality' we have another word, often used interchangeably with it, sometimes contrasted with it—I mean the word 'character'. This concept too we can bring into relation with the general scheme of Freudian psychology. Character can be explained as a disposition in the individual due to the repression of certain impulses which would otherwise be present in the personality; it is therefore something more restricted than personality. Character, which always has such a positive aspect, is really the result of certain fixities or negations imposed on the flow of consciousness. A flood only gains character and direction when it is confined between banks.

The word 'character' derives from the Greek word meaning an engraved sign, a distinguishing mark; and in common usage it always implies a man moulded to a pattern, firm, consistent, dependable. Again, the use of the word for that literary form known as 'the character' and practised by Theophrastus, Vauvenargues, and others, gives the same meaning: a consistent type. Descriptive psychologists adopt this same conception; the definition of Münsterberg may be quoted as typical. Character, he says, 'is the power to keep the selected motive dominant throughout life'. The difficulty about such a definition is that some 'power'—force, will, or energy—is implied, for which there is no adequate theory of causation. The psychoanalysts have supplied this, and again I think their hypothesis is the most suggestive one for our purposes. They regard inhibition as the basis of character, and a definition which we may accept as representative is that of Dr. Roback, which reads: '[Character is the result of] an enduring psycho-physical disposition to inhibit instinctive impulses in accordance with a regulative principle.' Now there are various words in that very condensed definition which need explanation. 'Inhibition' I have already referred to, but if we do not care to accept it in its psycho-analytical sense, I think it will do for our definition if we merely regard the 'disposition to inhibit' as the 'will to hold in check', in the ordinary moralistic sense. Again, the phrase 'instinctive impulses' need not be given any but its normal meaning—there are many instincts besides the sex instinct, and if any one instinct is more in question than another, I think it is probably the gregarious instinct.

This does not mean that the man who avoids the herd will thereby form his character; you do not inhibit an instinct by avoiding its activity. But the man who maintains a certain

integrity in the midst of the herd, that man is by way of form-
ing his character. Dr. Roback quotes very appositely Goethe's
couplet:

Es bildet ein Talent sich in der Stille:
Ein Charakter im Strome der Welt.

'A talent is formed in solitude; a character in the stream of the
world'—a sentiment which I would ask the reader to remember because I am presently going to suggest that this difference
between the conditions necessary for the formation of a
character and for the formation of what Goethe calls a talent
and what I am here calling a personality corresponds precisely
with the difference between rhetorical and lyrical literature,
which is the difference often loosely implied in the terms
'classical' and 'romantic' literature.

. . . Character is in fact armour against experience; it is not
in itself deflected by experience. From whatever direction we
approach it, we get the notion of fixity; and once a man's
character is determined, it is hardly possible to speak of his
moral or spiritual development. A character is 'set', 'hard-
boiled' as the slang phrase vividly expresses it. Not even the
emotions will dissolve it, or move it. The emotions indeed are
irrelevant to character; they are waves which break themselves
in vain against its base. History is full of examples of men of
character who have exercised their justness and firmness in
spite of the emotional claims of friendship and love.

Character, in short, is an impersonal ideal which the
individual selects and to which he sacrifices all other claims,
especially those of the sentiments or emotions. It follows that
character must be placed in opposition to personality, which
is the general common denominator of our sentiments and
emotions. That is, indeed, the opposition I wish to emphasize;
and when I have said further that all poetry, in which I
include all lyrical impulses whatsoever, is the product of the
personality, and therefore inhibited in a character, I have
stated the main theme of my essay.

. . . . .

24

But now we must enlarge our description of *personality*. As a preliminary I have suggested that the term might be identified with Freud's 'Ego'—a coherent organization of mental processes. But the coherence of this organization is not to be confused with the fixed organization of a character—any more than the coherence of a work of art is to be confused with the concision of a machine.

The ego is a synthesis of the sensations, is generated by conscious experience, by that inward perspective which Montaigne exercised so freely for our delectation. The judgement is not imposed on the sensations from without, as if by an external agency—that is the process of repression which results in character; judgement emerges from the history of our sensations, is elected by them, and the coherence of personality is indeed the coherence of a natural process; not the coherence of an arbitrary discipline.

... The personality is an active process of thought, a balance of relations maintained between our various feelings and sentiments. From this process, this play of thought, comes a certain act of belief, the *illative* act described by Newman. The nature of belief in general is not a subject to embark on now. I would merely suggest that the reality of the personality—its operative efficiency—is dependent on a belief in the existence of the self, a belief that may have little support in objective evidence, but is made possible by that insight into the future, that belief in the continuity of experience, which is the will to live. This is obviously a state of mind very different from that involved in character: the whole difference between blind compulsion to an external and arbitrary ideal and an organic coherence intuitively based on the actual world of sensation.

It looks, therefore, as though the one thing an artist must avoid is the fixity of character. This conclusion is forced on us from still another point of view. A man of character is generally distinguishable as a man of action.

· · · · · ·

If we say that there is a fundamental opposition between the artist and the man of action, the statement is acceptable enough. At least, it would fit typical artists like (to mention only poets) Shakespeare and Blake. It would explain the sudden withering of Wordsworth's genius: he acquired a character. But what of Milton and Goethe? Well, of Milton we can say that he was a poet of one kind in his youth, that he then became a man of action and was silent for twenty-five years, and then became a poet once more, but of a different kind. Of Goethe I cannot speak with any confidence, but I suspect that a complete analysis might reveal a real poet and a real personality, but a somewhat fictitious character. Finally—to repeat a suggestion I have already made—may we not perhaps explain the dreary quarrel of Romantic and Classic as an opposition between two kinds of art, springing respectively from character and from personality? It is an explanation that would work out very well in practice. We have only to think of Dryden and of Dr. Johnson, and to compare them with Shakespeare and Keats.

But then must we conclude, because a man of character is an admirable spectacle, in his fixity of demeanour and directness of action, a type to be envied and imitated, that therefore this other type of man, this mobile personality of which poets are made, can show no compensating virtues? Must we not rather conclude that the virtues of personality inhere in its very mobility? For though thought by its own nature is capable of logical development, it can be informed by the whole personality, and therefore made real, only when that personality is free to adapt itself to the movements of thought. Thought and personality go hand in hand, and their goal, whether confessed or not, is that state of vision or inspiration which all great spirits have attained.

Poetry is properly speaking a transcendental quality—a sudden transformation which words assume under a particular influence—and we can no more define this quality than we can define a state of grace. We can only make a number of distinctions, of which the main is the broad but elemental one between poetry and prose. I use the word 'elemental' deliberately, because I believe the difference between poetry and prose to be, not one of surface qualities, not of form in any sense, not even of *mode* of expression, but absolutely of essence. It is not a case of the mind, in need of expression, choosing between two ways—one poetry, the other prose. There is no choice for the particular state of mind in which poetry originates. It must either seek poetic expression or it must simply not be expressed; for an altogether lower tension, involving a different kind of mentality, must be substituted before the activity of prose expression can intervene.

All art originates in an act of intuition, or vision. But such *intuition* or vision must be identified with *knowledge* being fully present only when consciously objectified. This act of vision or intuition is, physically, a state of concentration or tension in the mind. The *process* of poetry consists firstly in maintaining this vision in its integrity, and secondly in expressing this vision in words. Words are generally (that is to say, in prose) the *analysis* of a mental state. But in the process of poetic composition words rise into the conscious mind as isolated objective 'things' with a definite equivalence in the poet's state of mental intensity. They are arranged or composed in a sequence of rhythm which is sustained until the mental state of tension in the poet is exhausted or released by this objective equivalence.

Words, their sound and even their very appearance, are, of course, everything to the poet: the sense of words is the sense of poetry. But words have associations carrying the mind beyond sound to visual image and abstract idea. And the poet, even as he becomes conscious of words in the act of composition, feels them tincturing his consciousness not only with sound, but also with colour and light and power—in short, with meaning. Poetry depends, not only on the sound of words, but even more on their mental reverberations.

A living language analyses into idioms: idioms are the live organisms of speech—words are molecules and letters atoms. Now this organic unit, this idiom, is instinct with rhythm; it has irrefrangible intonation, and poetic rhythm is but the extension and the aggregation of these primary rhythms. Even-measured, regularly accented verse is successful only in so far as it makes use of or accommodates itself to these idioms. Free verse, which includes the slightest as well as the widest divergence from regular pattern, is but the free use of these idioms.

Idioms arise out of the contacts of daily life. They are the response of the human organism to the elements around it. They reflect the speed of life, the pressure of life, its very essence. Idioms are the vocal chimings-in of man in the rhythm of life, and have their parallels in the beating of drums and the dancing of limbs. All the arts are built up from these primary elements, and their reality, their actuality, depends on this strict relation. To build up poetry with dead idioms is like living a life of dead habits and obsolete manners. But such is precisely the sickness of nearly all modern poetry: it rings false in the actual turmoil of the day.

We can only seize the real rhythm instinctively. It *has* been found—in the modern ballet, in American ragtime music, and in a minute quantity of modern poetry. But when we have found the rhythm we are only at the beginning of art. We have found no more than the instruments of art.

'It is not the observing of *Trochaicques* nor their *Iambicques* [writes Daniel in one place] that will make our writings ought the wiser: All their Poesie, all their Philosophie is nothing, unless we bring the discerning light of conceipt with us to apply it to use. It is not bookes, but onley that great booke of the world, and the all-overspreading grace of heaven that makes men truly judiciall.'

That warning against pedantry applies equally to the makers of new rhythms, for no amount of originality will benefit us if it lack 'the discerning light'. Technique we may learn from observations, but this final necessity is a gift of a more individual nature, depending not so much upon the influences of environment as upon an inborn capacity. Or, to speak more exactly, it depends upon a convergence of these two factors—upon the right mind co-operating with the finest sensibility, and then freely expressing itself.

Shakespeare is there to show us that tradition is a meaningless abstraction for the poet himself—'an irritable reaching after fact and reason'. Almost daily I lift my voice in thanksgiving for this immortal witness: a poet who was no pedant nor moralist, a man of no character nor convictions, of no caste nor culture, but just a naked sensibility living in its own gusto, reaching after nothing more distant than the impassioned accents of its own voice as it issued from the 'terrible crystal' of an intuitive mind.

The highest poetry is inconceivable without the intuition of pure being as well as the sense of existence. The poet must, if my contentions are right, live in the fleeting moments of vision, but in these moments his vision penetrates very deep and far, and the degree of its penetration is measured by the range of the poet's thought or intelligence. And so, indeed, is the coherence of his personality, for 'thought is guaranteed by its own laws'. It is always an essay in order, in clarification; and that is why it cannot accept the dogmas of character, which would limit its range, or at least confine it to one direction. But the range—the ranging searchlight—of the intelligence, its essential mobility, is not to be confused with the vagaries of pseudo-romanticism, or any theory of poetry which presupposes the primacy of sentiment; poetry as the direct expression of sentiment.

There is not one literary tradition, but many traditions; there is certainly a romantic tradition as well as a classical tradition, and, if anything, the romantic tradition has the longer history. As I see the problem, it is again a question of intelligence—of that intelligence which operates spontaneously whenever the personality is free. It is merely a lack of intelligence to refuse the experience embodied in the poetry of the past; but it shows an even greater lack of intelligence to refuse the experience embodied in the present. The only duty which the poet has in this matter is to refuse his allegiance to academic cadres. But if we must apply the historical distinctions to this age of ours, we shall find ourselves in a dilemma, for we shall be forced to admit that, whilst it is possibly an age of satiety, it is not one of solidity; and if it is certainly an age of stress, we are more doubtful about its energy. That is to say, it is not clearly either a romantic or a classical age, nor are the categories of a romantic or a classical tradition applicable to it. In the circumstances the poet has no alternative but to rely on 'a certain inward perspective', a coherence of the personality based on the widest evidence of the senses. I am aware that I shall be accused of merely dressing up the old romanticism in new phrases; but forced into this academic discussion I might then accept 'the rehabilitation of romanticism' as an adequate description of my aims.

ALEX COMFORT

AN EXPOSITION
OF IRRESPONSIBILITY

I N its September–October 1942 issue *Partisan Review* adver-
tised a number to be devoted to the discussion of certain
tendencies of thought which it described as obscurantist.
These include the abandonment of the historical for the metaphysical approach to ethics and politics, the belief in the concept of original sin, and the denial of historical progress as an
inevitable development. In the generation of English writers
from 1938 onwards, the writers whose first significant work has
appeared since European war was declared, the concepts which
you mention are becoming gradually more and more the
guiding principles of both thought and art. Belonging to that
generation myself, I am personally conscious of the influence
of these assertions and denials in my own experience: I am
unable to regard them as retrograde. We have passed so
recently through a period of classicism, in which the historical
and scientific approach was made the basis of poetry, that we
are in a position to realize some at least of its limitations. I am
unable to find any comparable classicism in recent American
poetry, except in so far as it is derived from Auden.

I should first explain what positive view I hold of the nature
of the historical process in art. I regard the periods of English
Literature as an alternation between the classical and the
romantic outlook on thought and on writing. It is as if the
awareness of the significance of death as a factor in interpretative art became alternately emphasized and obscured. The
classical periods are periods of security, economic and mental,
where the drive is towards action and where the majority of
the people are in possession of a satisfactory interpretation of
the universe and of themselves, provided either by religion

or by political theory. They are periods in which the burden of realizing and interpreting the conflict between factual death and the human desire for the permanent devolves upon single artists, who tend to become major poets. The Victorian period was one such, and it produced its Arnolds and Mark Rutherfords who agonized within the structure of its prejudice as much, quantitatively if not qualitatively, as did Rimbaud or Rilke in their own periods, or Unamuno and Lorca in contemporary Europe. The active periods with their extroverted public alternate regularly with periods in which the realization of human tragedy becomes generalized. In these times the *individual* experience of men like Unamuno becomes the general property not only of the majority of artists but of the majority of mankind. Major poetry, which is the vicarious function of the single artist, who takes upon himself the weight of human tragic awareness in order to shield humanity at large from its realization, becomes quite impossible. I rather doubt if at any time in history so many ordinary individuals have realized the personal reality of death as realize it today. We are at present in the period of transition from a major period of classicism (Victorian) which produced in its turn romantic poets as individuals and finally classical poets employing the husk of romantic technique. Slack water was at about 1900, and the silence of serious art in England enabled Georgianism, a relative valley, to pass itself off as a peak. Monro couldn't understand why everyone was silent, and he shouted to fill the gap. There were two attempts to reinstate a classical approach, one in which rules still apply: the Imagists with their increasing tragic awareness, and the Audenites who expressly attempted to deny the reality of that awareness. The importance of Auden to the present generation is in the assertion which he made that history is amenable to reason, and his discovery in experience that it is not. If the Spanish war was the occasion of this discovery it was not the cause. Those poets who stayed at home, or who were too young to benefit from that historical demonstration, came to exactly the same conclusion in walking about the streets of London in the course of their normal and personal activities. I don't feel that it is profitable to attempt to locate finally the point in literature in which the transition took place. Some writers have pointed to Dylan Thomas—yet his awareness of death, on his own showing, dates from childhood, at a time when he was not consciously elaborating any sort of poetic experience. The question is not one of sudden transition—it is a matter of the relative numbers of those who have arrived at a frame of mind. Artists can reflect it because it is the general temper of the public, or they can explore it vicariously for the public, as doctors explore disease.

I am emphasizing this quasi-priestly function which I feel that poets frequently fill, and the awareness of death rather than the awareness of life not out of a personal morbidity, but because to anyone who is in contact with English writers at the moment they are omnipresent features. Like some evolutionary changes in genetics, this realization occurs generally throughout a culture, not spreading from person to person by discussion or example, but arising in a number of places at once. In part this is the result of the general course of history, but there seems to be some less concrete influence at work. So that although one may have been elaborating the ideas in isolation, and one accepts them as *intellectual* concepts, they are emotionally conditioned. When one comes to talk to another artist who has been arriving, also in isolation, at the same ideas, one encounters a repetition of personal experience.

The conclusions which *Partisan Review* described as 'obscurantist', and which have driven us to the conscious pursuit of romanticism, are these:

1. That history is not to be regarded as a steady progress in any direction, whether morally or politically defined, e.g. civilization, goodness, socialism, but as an oscillation about a fixed point, an ebb and flow between certain fixed limits which are never exceeded. We feel very strongly that no other sort of interpretation of recorded history is reasonable. It is impossible to suggest to us that man is either morally better or politically closer to a state which does not involve the abuse

of power. His achievement fluctuates sufficiently for us to say that democracy is 'better' than fascism, or Athens in 400 B.C. preferable to Rome in A.D. 50, but the statement that absolute qualitative change has taken place between 500 B.C. and A.D. 1942 has no meaning for us.

2. That because we have no belief in immortality we are not able to find any intellectual significance in human life comparable to that which the Christian (or the Marxist) finds.[1] Accordingly we accept a purely human analysis of history in preference to a supernatural one. We are concerned to discover the sort of principles which underlie human thought and belief as revealed in comparative sociology and in the myth, and to elaborate them as guides to our own art and conduct.

3. That one of these principles or properties common to humanity is the congenital inability not to abuse power when incorporated into any sort of body. This is roughly speaking the doctrine of original sin, but it has no mystical basis and there is no corresponding doctrine of grace. One does not detect this tendency in every individual when he acts individually, but the larger the group the more obvious the tendency. One can compare human associations to boats filled with blindfold rowers—the positive influences which would tend to goodwill or unselfishness cancel out (the boat makes no progress) but the negative and disruptive impulses summate (she sinks under the weight of her collected crew). We differ as to the degree to which education can redirect or eradicate these impulses, but we tend, I think, to feel that cultivation of the *negative* impulse is considerably easier than that of the positive (a fact which general human experience seems to admit—it is notoriously easier to be antisocial than social, or we should have our Utopia on a plate, and all languages traditionally compare deterioration to a journey *down* hill). Our political attitude is modified by this belief. It

[1] There is no room here to go into the eschatology of Marxism—I have done so elsewhere; but it seems to me to assume a system of ethics based on absolute statements while denying the principle of absolutes—in other words it preaches an altruism which it fails to justify by reason and is unwilling to regard as emotional.

owes something, but not much, to the corresponding Calvin-
ism of Niebuhr and Karl Barth, and it recognizes a pene-
trating allegorical statement of the impasse in Genesis, where
man's inability to live up to his principles is made to coincide
with his discovery of the principles themselves. But this is not
in any sense a religious belief. Politically it involves the rejection of democracy, because the majority is consistently wrong,
a priori; it also involves the rejection of fascism, because
fascism is nothing more nor less than the attempt to use the
negative impulses in man as a cohering force, a sort of Sweden-
borgian hell by common consent. We should be fascists only if
we believed that the differences between positive and negative
human impulses were irrelevant. The only defensible ethic is
the ethic of community in misfortune, of unity and mutual aid
against a hostile environment. There are for us no principles
outside man, no standard but humanness. Accordingly there
remains to us only anarchism, though not of the kind which
believes in the perfectibility of human nature. In conclusion,
we recognize in ourselves all the symptoms which we describe
in others.

For now politically we regard ourselves as absolved. The
state, having consistently shown itself to be evil, in so far as we
understand at all what 'evil' means, has absolved us by its
idiocy. We now bear and accept no responsibility to any group,
to any body for its own sake, not even to ourselves, but only
to individuals. Every bond that in past times held the single
man, the sane man, to the allegiance of groups is for us nulli-
fied. Since association and incorporation can only aggravate
the evil tendencies which lead to the abuse of power, it is our
intention to regard as void all such associations. Those who
join voluntarily or by compulsion in them have constructed
worlds for themselves in which we have no part at all. We can
only regard them as negative. Accordingly we now *are* our own
rulers and our own governments—our politics have been
thoroughly atomized. There are no corporate allegiances any
longer, only individuals and groups, committed to a general
human responsibility at continual variance with the corporate,

and with all who are prepared to delegate their minds, whether to a single ruler or to a committee of rulers. That is to say, we are each of us, intellectually though not practically, a one-man nation. It looks as though the sole remaining factor standing between the possibility of living a sane life and its destruction by lunatics is the disobedience of the individual.

There is only one reasonable interpretative task for the artist in contemporary society. He has placed on him the entire burden of speaking for the voiceless. Most human beings are robbed of their voices either by force or by fraud, and the artist, who keeps his own precariously, has a responsibility which outweighs all the alleged 'irresponsibility' of his attitude to maniacal institutions. The weak of this world, the raw material from which both the hostages and the firing squad, the airman and his civilian victims, the Indian and the fellows who flop him, are recruited, are the people to whom I personally feel a responsibility. And when the sufferings of one or another are held up as a bait to induce me to inflict further suffering on others, all I can reasonably do is disobey, and lend the victims my voice. Modern literature is full of such borrowed voices—not hard-luck stories, mind you, but voices—of the soldiers who are muzzled, the people whose sons are taken, the decent folk who are led up the garden path—and, since they have undergone the final indignity, of the dead. Responsible writers are the diametrical opponents of the Goebbelses and Brackens of this world whose aim is to deprive men of speech. It is in this field that we redeem our irresponsibility.

This is an outlook which is forced upon us partly by history and partly by the conclusions we have reached concerning the nature and character of man. It is illogical in that it does not even provide for an efficient corporate town drainage. But in a nation at war it is, for the artist, the only workable way of living. However illogical it is, all other attitudes seem more so. We are deriving perpetual benefit from the society which we are trying to deny, but we can do no other. It should be stressed that we are aware of the extent to which our attitude depends upon the things which it renounces for its food and livelihood. But both in a wartime democracy or in a totalitarian state this same atomization is an almost inevitable process for all those who value interpretative art or intellectual liberty. It is incorrect to suggest that we have *seceded* from society. It has ejected us, by its refusal to grant the fundamental conditions which we are entitled to lay down in the capacity of artists. At present we are living on in English society partly without the landlord's knowledge and partly because he is too kind-hearted to chuck us out. It is not possible to see at present which way the historical trends will go.

E. F. F. HILL

APOCALYPSE

I

Apocalypse affirms the freedom of the human spirit, man's sonship and co-partnership with the divine in the transfiguration and redemption of the world and in the resurrection of the dead. It acknowledges the freedom of man to reject the divine principle, to send God to the devil and to enclose himself within the solitude of hell. To deny Apocalypse is to deny that man has access, in his own right and of his own freedom, to the inner spiritual sources of being. It is also to deny that man may, again of his own right and of his own freedom, sunder himself from these sources and live self-contained and perfectly happy in the torments of the solitude of hell. It is not to deny the existence of these sources, but to make them external to and independent of the world historical process; that is, to put God at a distance from the world, and to substitute concepts and abstract propositions for the life of the spirit. An abstract proposition is never a statement of the truth, neither is it a sufficient ground upon which to base an inquiry into the truth.

The theme of Apocalypse is, therefore, death and hell, the meaning of which it discloses. In that death is its theme, it is concerned with the tragic destiny of man in the world. In that hell is its theme, it is concerned with the tragedy of man in his freedom, with the tragedy of the person in its deepest and most acute form. Man may achieve victory over death and over time, may rise from the dead and, being risen, may enjoy the torments of hell 'for ever'. But 'for ever' is infinity and not eternity. Eternity has nothing to do with infinity. There is an infinite instant and an eternal instant, and in both there is victory over time: in the former it is a victory achieved by the self for the self regardless of an other, as if there was no other; in the latter it is a victory achieved by the self for an other, for at least one other, and this is a victory over hell.

The theme of Apocalypse is the crisis of Spirit.

II

Apocalypse is active, but there are passive apocalyptic moods. These have one common cause, although they differ much in their summing-up of the historical process and in their account of man's position in it. They derive from a drying-up of the sources from which man has nourished his spiritual life and, in consequence, they reflect a fear of freedom and the desire to throw off its burden. There is an oppressive feeling of anxiety which nothing in the world can relieve. The self is imprisoned in the world. And the world is utterly without meaning and trivial. Here, the possibility of the co-operation of man in his freedom with God in his freedom in creative activity of any kind is denied. Indeed, freedom is denied both to man and to God, for man can do no other than await the coming horror, the divinely fated destruction of the world, and God must act under the binding necessity of a righteous anger. It is not the principle of freedom which here enters into righteousness and judgement, but fear. And the fear of God is more terrible than the fear of man. God becomes his own evil and a darkness which engulfs the world. The principle of justice is dominant, but it is abstract. The principle of love is absent. Every evil thing brings death into the world. Of this there cannot be two opinions. And evil things are in the world. But these passive apocalyptic moods can recognize no ground for the redemption and transfiguration of evil. Death is not an enemy to be overcome, but a punishment to be endured. The historical process is swallowed up in death. Death is the meaning of life.

III

There are active apocalyptic moods which are false. Here the human principle is divorced from the divine in a manner no less absolute than is the case where the moods are passive. But whereas there the human is discredited, here it assumes the prerogatives of the divine. This is so even in the case where a man takes the decisive step of renouncing the evil world with the avowed object of discovering God in the depths of his own being. He forsakes the forsaken world and leaves it to its doom. But he cannot step out of the historical process, however thoroughgoing his introversion may be. Neither does his introversion throw any light upon the meaning of history, or of himself in the world and upon the point of forsaking the world now and not at some other time, here and not in some other place. This is a condition of acute self-consciousness, and it remains so even at the moment (should such a moment ever come) when he plunges into the blinding darkness of the mystical abyss of absolute oneness with 'the Universal Spirit'. It is a condition which expresses the disharmony which exists between himself and the world and his inability to resolve it. He declares his dislike of the world. He pronounces judgement upon the world and upon the meaninglessness of the world. Yet his withdrawal from the world is something which takes place in the world and something which happens to the world. It reflects the inner destiny of the world; the world is forsaken and given over to evil. What, in effect, he does forsake is not the world but an idea of the world. The world as being God-forsaken is never the judgement of those who love the world but of those who, from whatever motive, hate the world. These men are unable to go beyond their discrete and individual state and, sundered from God, they assume the prerogatives of God.

God is to be discovered in the depths of man's being, but another must be the searcher and not he. Man is in the world as the bearer of its meaning, even when he hides himself in the innermost reaches of his subjective being. Every man,

without exception, is in the world as the bearer of its meaning
—to another who will search until he finds it in him, but never
to himself. Meaning is disclosed not as an answer to any
question how? or what? or why? which man may ask, and not
in any objective or subjective mode, but as the creative
response of God to man's own creative activity. On the one
hand, it is the communion of man with the content of God's
knowledge of being and, on the other, it is the communion of
God with man's knowledge of being. There cannot be revelation, that is, a disclosure of meaning, if there is a rift between
the two. And by communion I mean something much closer
than 'entering into' and 'sharing'. The instant of disclosure is
an apocalyptic instant. It is also an eternal instant.

It is not possible to set too high a value upon the worth of
any man, even upon the 'worthless'. But it is according to the
degree in which we succeed in uncovering dignity and honour
in another that we have sufficient ground to affirm it of ourselves. There is a place upon this earth where I may stand in
heaven; it is wherever I chance upon another, for he comes
towards me as the creation of the Wisdom of God, the bearer
of the divine meaning of the world and of death and hell, of
evil and good, of slavery and freedom, and of life. If, when I
meet him, I see only the demonic, if I see nothing noble but
only banal and sordid things, the task is set me—not to senti-
mentalize and slobber over him—to uncover the divine and
thus reveal the human. This is man's supreme engagement.
War in heaven is in myself whenever and wherever I chance
upon another and nowhere else. The apocalyptic symbol bears
directly upon this. Sundered from the spiritual sources of
being and sundered within the self, man's struggle is for
personality.

But I cannot struggle for personality by and for myself. I
cannot be a person; I can be none other than an individual
sundered part save as I am at one with my fellow men—the
meanest and the noblest—in our common oneness with God.
The achievement of personality implies triumph over the sickness of individuality. It is the victory of man in his freedom

over egoism, over the spirit which denies the worth of another, of any other, which cannot break through the condition of particularity, over the spirit of hell. Man's position in the world is tragic not because he cannot find God, but because God cannot find him, because he hides himself from God. And when God does discover man, he is found crucified, subjected to torture, ignominy and death at the hands of those who affirm God but deny man to God, that is, deny the freedom of God's search for and approach to man. Atheism is not primarily the denial of God, but the denial of man in the presence of God. The achievement of personality is the victory of the Holy Spirit, and the Holy Spirit is none other than the spirit of Communism. But here I anticipate, for to state the matter thus is to face the ultimate problem of universal history. It is according to the degree in which we live in others in our freedom and others live in us in their freedom that we know ourselves to be the centre of the universe. An egoist can be, to himself, none other than a point upon the circumference.

When a man turns away from the world with a view to forsaking the world because it is fallen and evil and terror-ridden, he turns away from God, for all that is mean and evil in the world is the Wisdom of God, and every uttered word, every curse and blasphemy is the Word of God, every thought the Logos of God, distorted and debased, waiting its redemption, waiting the apocalyptic instant. When a man creeps into himself, away from the world and fertilizes himself, he dies to the doom of the world and from himself brings forth a new heaven and a new earth, both strictly private. He does achieve victory over death but hell is enlarged. He has shaped for his highest good a world in which he may go unhindered upon his own solitary sovereign way. Like the white horseman of the Apocalypse he rides forth, with a crown upon his pate, conquering and to conquer. He dies to the doom of the world; he cannot rise to the redemption and transfiguration of the world.

IV

The fundamental antithesis which is disclosed in the tragic unfolding of the historical process is not between spirit and matter, nor yet between good and evil; it is not between the divine and the demonic, but between freedom in the truth and fear of the truth. There would be no historical as distinct from the cosmogonic process if each and every man was not capable of recognizing and making actual the truth. This recognition and actualization is the perfection of his potentialities. Truth, not as an object of search or knowledge, not as relating to any partial state, whether of time as concerning the past or as anticipating the future, or of space as setting a value upon the extended relatedness of mutually exclusive things, but truth as the direct unmediated apprehension and assimilation of the rhythmic unity of the Whole, is of the very essence of the structure of man's consciousness. This is explicitly the divine image which each man bears, and is the ground of his absolute worth. But for this there could be no Apocalypse, no disclosure of meaning. Thus it is that the concept 'individuality' is inadequate and false in relation to man and to history, however useful it may be in determining his position in the cosmogonic process. The goal of the historical process is the achievement of personality, and this implies freedom in the truth. Thus, the person is not a means to any end whatsoever, neither is he a part of any whole. He is the whole; he is the whole-in-God. I am the whole-in-God; thou art the whole-in-God; we are the whole-in-God.

It would be a foolish blunder to assume that an identity of grammatical structure implies an actual identity. There is no identity here, no similarity, no repetition, but uniqueness. The divine image which I bear and which another must uncover is unique and irreplaceable and is my creative contribution. The divine image which another bears and which I must uncover is unique and irreplaceable and is his creative contribution. Creative activity is polar; it is the rhythmic unity of two opposing principles: on the one hand my bearing the divine image and on the other my disclosure of the divine image which another bears. When these are sundered there are both the incommunicable madness of the lonely individual and the all-togetherness of the collective. And the conflict between the two is the Apocalyptic Armageddon. Personality is the achievement of their rhythmic unity.

There is an active apocalyptic mood which associates itself with theories of progress and evolution. It thus confuses the historical with the cosmogonic process, and oftentimes expresses itself in terms of a mixture of the two, especially in its understanding of time and in its treatment of death. There is no fated end to the world; if the world does end in catastrophe then it will be because man has not exerted himself sufficiently to overcome the irrational forces which are in him, and has not applied with sufficient care the means which he has developed and is always improving for the mastery of nature. Mastery over man and mastery over nature are the two chief means of achieving the desired goal—unending human happiness in a world of plenty from which evil has been legislated away. And as mastery over nature is almost an automatic process, it is to mastery over man that attention must be given. Everything depends upon the activity of man and careful planning. The world is plastic; man is free to shape it according to his determined ends. This gives definition to the scope of freedom. Matter is endowed with the qualities of spirit: it has its own dialectic. It would be a mistake to dismiss this out of hand as a piece of muddled thinking. It expresses a hope and a faith which should not be ignored. Impenetrability is not among the order of unchangeable things. Man can overcome it. But man is not so plastic as the world, nor so *rational* as matter. Therefore . . . it is in the conclusion which it draws and in the steps which it takes to implement it that this mood is false. Man must be dragged to happiness by force, made to march to future bliss under police and military guard, impelled by the grim discipline of an artificially created want.

Everything which has taken place in the world so far is meaningless and full of corruption and deceit. *So far*: there is the naïve belief that the present is always superior to the past and the moment hence superior to the present; that somewhere among the onrushing moments of the future there is one supreme moment which will bring with it the cancelling out of corruption and deceit. The past is discredited. Man is an individual, a part of a whole. The individual is born. The individual dies. The processes which are herein involved are clearly understood and may be legislated for. Death is trivialized and ignored. The individual has no intrinsic value. Value resides in the collective; the collective does not die. The hope of the future is based upon the death of the present—of the individual, of an epoch. Hence death is welcomed. Man, the individual, is treated not as one who is creatively active in the unfolding of the historical process, but as a product of the cosmogonic process, as an experiment in whom there is no unity of consciousness with previous experiments, to be himself overpassed and forgotten. He is held fast within the limitations of a finite natural process which has no regard for its particulars. In so far as he is free—and freedom together with justice, solidarity and love for humanity are not uncommon expressions of this apocalyptic mood—he is like the three blind mice, free to choose what he must choose under pain of liquidation. The unfolding of higher from lower forms, the uncovering of meaning, the unity of consciousness in the transition from past to present from present to future, the right and value of all present thought and action are in the secret councils of the few and are incomprehensible to him. He is not encouraged to know more than is necessary to the efficient discharge of his assigned function. He is to be understood and valued in terms of his function; that is, his value rests upon grounds which are relative to a collective purpose —the reaching of a far-off and invisible goal. Fear and control of the spoken and printed word are used as means to ensure this. He is definitely encouraged to possess an isolated consciousness. He is not permitted to have a general consciousness. Not only may he not be free in the truth but, upon pain of death, he may not choose to know the truth. His life has meaning only in obedience, labour and death, but upon his death will the future happiness of the world be based. He must be overpassed.

A study of the laws of nature discloses that a man has but a short time to live and a shorter time to labour and produce, and that the generation of the sons takes over where the generation of the fathers leaves off. The generation of the fathers is immortalized in the generation of the sons. But this is not quite accurate, for the felicity of the generation of the fathers is lost to the generation of the sons. It is the labour of the generation of the fathers which is immortalized in the labour of the generation of the sons. The generation of the mothers waters the earth with its tears for the futility of the pains of its labour and is immortalized as the resting-place of the deceased generations of the fathers. All the generations of men are immortalized not in the far-off goal, but in the infinite recession of the goal, in the ceaseless striving to stay an insatiable longing. Immortality is in time. It is the invisible moment hence, the inexhaustible torrent of moments hence which sweeps upon the present to destroy it. Immortality is the incurable wound of sundered, fractured time. But sundered time is itself a symbol of a sundering within the consciousness of man, of disintegration of being. It is really nonsense to speak of time as sundered; time has no past, present or future. It is man's inner sundered, sexual and uprooted being which reflects its torn and fretful state upon outer circumstance, which buries the past, heeds not the present and deifies the future. The only solution of universal history is in the healing of the wounds of man's inner sundered state and in regaining contact with the spiritual sources of being. It is to this that the apocalyptic symbol points. Apocalypse does not speak of immortality but of resurrection and eternal life.

V

Apocalypse has nothing to say about the 'march of progress', the funeral march of slaves.

Apocalypse differs from all theories of progress in that it affirms the intrinsic value of each who has ever lived and of his participation in and contribution to the solution of universal history. It affirms his death, it affirms also his resurrection from the dead. It reserves for him, no matter to what 'period of time' he may belong, the disclosure of meaning, the solution of history. Apocalypse is neither optimistic nor pessimistic. Its vision is entire. Theories of progress thrive upon the disintegration of being and deny the past save as it has served as a means to the present. Revolution is resurrection (into time, not into eternity): the denied and forgotten dead rise in revolt against the oppressive present. But it does not bring with it the power to heal the wounds of division, the sickness of disintegration. It is war between the sundered parts. It is a disjunction of consciousness. Revolution has its own theory of progress.

The action of Apocalypse is ruthless. It is penetration into the darkest hide-out, the tearing off of every mask, the ripping up of every respectability, the overturning of every morality, the exposure of every secret thing. One may no longer speak of the unconscious, the subconscious, the conscious and the superconscious; these are formal divisions and are overpassed. There is only the unity of consciousness. There is not an obscenity, not a deceit, not a crime, not a sordid triviality, not a cry, not a despair which is not exposed to view. None is permitted to become a world to itself. Apocalypse is incredible. Life is incredible. History is incredible. Man is incredible. God is incredible. All is incredible. The book sealed with seven seals, which is the book of history, is filled with such incredible horror that 'no man in heaven, nor in earth, neither under the earth, was able to open the book, neither to look thereon' save 'the Lamb that was slain'. And at the opening of the seventh seal, heaven itself is frozen into silence at the disclosed horrors which involve the cosmogonic with the historic process. But it is not a non-human principle, not a universal will before which man is powerless or against which he must wage war, which is the operating cause. Every human action is a seed; every seed bears fruit; every fruit must be eaten. The ancient insight which discloses this much of the truth cannot be ignored. Man, depolarized, civilized, moral, respectable, good, efficient, just, giving the worth of the whole to his sundered parts, speeds across the world conquering and to conquer, to starve and to kill.

When we idealize a fragment, even though the fragment be the last remaining sign of dignity, the process of disintegration has gone far. The end is death. We shout glory because infamy surrounds us and we ourselves are infamous, honour because of dishonour, dignity because of meanness, purity because of filth, greatness because of sordid triviality. There is no entire vision. We are caught up in a process; not a cosmogonic process but a spiritual process, a process of decomposition, and are its playthings: we have surrendered to it; we have surrendered to death. We shout for humanity, sacrifice the generations and ourselves, turn every nook and cranny into a Golgotha, nail ourselves to crosses of our own making because we loathe men and women and bury ourselves in the dust of dead systems.

The disclosure of horror is not an entire vision. The incredible thing about the Apocalypse is the passion of spirit which breaks into song. Harps and crowns and white robes and pavements of gold and walls of crystal and the light of the sun and the River of Life are doubtless naïve symbols to men who cannot get away from rusting iron and broken machinery and slagheaps and syphilis and bombs and poison gas and deserts and fear and the smell of death. The symbols matter little before the passion of the spirit which breaks into song. The horror *and* the song, the great Whore *and* the Bride, evil *and* good, death *and* life polarized, in rhythmic wholeness; the horror, the Whore, evil and death transfigured and redeemed.

It is here that the meaning of death and hell is disclosed and the dignity and majesty of man is established, 'for since by man came death, by man came also the resurrection of the dead'.

Death *and* resurrection from the dead is the only way by which a man may overcome his sundered depolarized state and triumph over hell. Hell is the condition of depolarized man who cannot die. The inability to die is of the sweet tormenting pleasures of hell. So also is the inability to love. Death is not the denial of infinity but its affirmation. Death is the denial of the life of the person, that is, of eternal life. The achievement of personality is victory over death and hell. Death is the lot of individuality and is part of the cosmogonic process. But personality is not part of any such process. Birth confers individuality; individuality cannot be avoided. Personality is not conferred. It is a creation. It is also a creative act. It is the ability to worship the worth of another. Death is not a tragedy for the individual; it is its inevitable end. Death is a tragedy only when there is awareness of personality, and then because of the loss or the fear of the loss of the worth of another, which means the shattering of the unity of one's own consciousness. Love for all that lives involves the anguish of the struggle against death for the sake of the worth of at least one other. To do what a man may do for any end whatsoever, whether it be base or exalted, which does not include the worship of the worth of another is death; it is the definition of death. It is part of a process of the disintegration of being. Love for another may be transformed to love for an idea, for an abstract good. It is when this happens that Satan falls from heaven and his vexatious journeyings to and fro upon the earth begin. It is a mistake to think that evil is irrational; it rationalizes freedom. To mine coal, to bake bread, to remove mountains, to dam rivers, to cross seas, to civilize savages—each is a task easy to define, but death is its end, its summing-up, its meaning unless it is done as worship of the worth of another. Thus it is that man is enslaved both to the machine which he has made to master nature and to nature, and also to the social norm which he has established. The machine, nature (the cosmogonic process), and society become instruments of death. It is man's task, well within the range of the perfection of his potentialities, to redeem nature, the machine, and society. This is the new element in consciousness, the new enrichment of the truth, the new war in heaven. It is crisis of Spirit. It is not a question of the victory of good over evil, of justice over injustice, of equality over inequality. Such trifling matters are not involved. It is a question of triumph over death; whether man will be free in the truth thus enriched (without shadow of turning or compromise) or succumb to fear of the truth, and seek refuge behind an overpassed horizon.

But man does not redeem nature by improving it, nor the machine by perfecting it, nor yet society by reforming it, but by reversing the process of the disintegration of being of which his own depolarized state is the deep ground.

Whatever a man does as worship of the worth of another, of all others, is triumph over death, and the redemption of the instruments of his toil. Freedom in the truth together with the worship of the worth of all others is of the essence of the spirit of Communism. It is the definition of the Holy Spirit. A deflection from this, to howsoever slight a degree, leads to tyranny and death.

The crowning symbol of the Apocalypse, the Lamb and his Bride, is that of sexual love, the uncovering and affirmation of the worth of another; the healing of the wounds of conflict between depolarized sundered parts. Hell is vanquished; death is overcome in this and in no other way. Upon the instant that a man uncovers the dignity and honour of another and so lives in that other that he worships the worth of all others, he justifies in himself the historical process, is himself its goal and its meaning, and lives the eternal life, even though his body twist, upon the instant following, with the torment of disease and die. Energy from a higher plane of existence has broken through the closed order of finite relationships and transfigured it. He lives the eternal life; he is the first and the last; he it is 'that liveth and was dead and is alive for evermore'. He holds the keys of hell and of death. God is revealed upon earth.

WALFORD MORGAN

NOTES ON CONTEMPORARY
TENDENCIES

THE APOCALYPTIC SCHOOL

IN our time there are so many factors in one's consciousness
of which one is not fully aware, so many factors which will
emerge into the full light of reason only when they have
begun to lose their real potency, so many intuitive needs which
will be adequately expressed only when they have been
resolved, that when one finds oneself face to face with the
increasing stream of modern verse, one hesitates to embark
upon definite conjecture, or to make any immediate prophecy
about the qualities it will display in the future.

Some observations however can be made. For we have seen
within the last few years in poetry a complete volte-face both
in manner of treatment and in objective. The mood of inspiration too has largely changed. The 1930's thought that poetry
and art could revolutionize life. It is recognized now that it is
much truer to say that it is life that changes art; and that each
decade evokes its own particular qualities and vices. The
moods of Picasso, for instance, it can be seen, and the vigorous
disharmonies of Bartok are so much an expression of our
Zeitgeist that they resume more effectively than any philosophy the underlying spirit and temper of the day; and have
in a sense the defects of their era. To change the 'Portrait
d'une dame, 5 mars 1940' of Picasso or his 'Femme au costume
vert, février 1940', one would need to alter the underlying
circumstances and troubles of the age—the broken ties, the
uprooted friendships and marriages, and the faulty values

which have found their outlet in the chaos of two wars. For it is through the broken facets of modern life, of disharmony and discord, that the acute vision of Picasso finds visual expression. The price the poet has to pay for real activity is that of contemporaneity and awareness. Poetry in order to be created has to be created out of the complex of direct or intuitive perceptions and apprehensions which form the poet's consciousness, and which come to him as an active member of a living community. That is why the artist has often been called the flickering gauge-reading of the thoughts and minds of his time. And if the outward world is sick and disordered, the community diseased, the poet suffers from an acute form of anguish and is set with problems of expression and adjustment. Often it is imperative that he be a revolutionary.

Each decade has constantly to find the satisfaction of newly felt and inherent needs which were probably subordinated and only half-realized in previous modes of expression—has to find new orientations and new directions. In the unsatisfactory world of today it is natural that such should be the case; and that movements should lead poetry through many different phases. Just as painting has passed through Post-impressionism, Cubism, and Surrealism (to mention but a few phases which could be multiplied were we to cast our mind over the movements in different countries), so too, modern poetry has developed a highly sensitive consciousness not only of progress in the other visual arts but of the whole trends and movements in European thought in our time. That perhaps will prove to be one of the outstanding characteristics of the poetry of our day. It is true to say in a special sense that English verse has never been the same since the advent of Hofmannsthal and Rilke (to a lesser degree one might add George) and since Baudelaire, Mallarmé, and Rimbaud; all poets who can roughly be classified (Baudelaire alone excepted) under the general trends of symbolism. For tendencies now appear to be internationally rather than nationally traditional; the cross-fertilization of the cultures of various countries being a factor of the utmost significance for literature in our time.

That is not quite the same thing as saying that regional or national movements will be subordinated beneath general international trends; but rather that regional and national cultures which find their expression in poetry—Welsh, Spanish, Chinese, German, etc.—while retaining their inherent qualities, will now feel themselves increasingly enriched by a consciousness of a similar inward struggle that goes on everywhere else under the diverse operations of the Spirit, throughout all mankind; and will find themselves in the forefront of man's battle for freedom. Differences of race and nationality, of religion and culture, will give each language its own tonalities, naturally, and its own peculiar texture, its own particular emotional and metaphysical range; differences which in ultimate essence will always be untranslatable; but there will often be an identity of aims.

These factors being predominantly operative, within this complex of influences one can discern two distinctive phases in recent English poetry; both aiming at different qualities and achieving different ends; apparent in two decades.

In Auden, Day Lewis, and Spender—and more particularly in their followers in the 30's—a new proletarian consciousness came into being; one saw the current of modern verse nourished by the effluvia of many a factory; the downward reaches tinged by the tainted by-products of a predominantly materialistic age; the swans of poetry swimming in an iridescence of oil. The meticulous accuracy of the technologist acquired such a prestige value that it turned the poetry of the decade into the photographic reportage of the journalist. And brilliant though these chief protagonists were, it was undoubtedly a phase in which the spirit was fettered. In spite of many an inward conflict and the desire to show the supremacy of human values, it was the outward and mechanical creation of man that was honoured. Salvation was to come, according to the trite formula—a formula soon to be overdone and refuted—through the triumph of technology. It was a movement which was primarily logical and rational in its manner and at the same time ideological in its aims. Its strength and its weakness derived equally from the fact that it identified itself ideally with a community—that of the Russian Communist state; and from that factor derived a large measure of unity.

It was inevitable that a reaction should set in; and stress be laid upon personal as opposed to sociological values; that emphasis should be placed upon the unfettered growth and development of the human spirit. Poetry acquired thereby a more fruitful field of operation; enriched itself by claiming purposefully a new liberty and a new dimension. The emphasis which had been laid upon schemes for the proletarian state now brought to light an essential defect; revealed the need for the primacy of the things of the spirit. The inward and spiritual life of man was realized afresh to be of more ultimate value than the finest schemes of Marxist dialectical materialism. In other words, the desired truths propounded by the earlier outlook having been assimilated, a new revaluation seemed necessary. Hope now was felt to lie increasingly in the realization by man of his real and spiritual destiny and purpose.

This reaction was most cogently formulated in the Anarchism of Herbert Read, who, sensing the revaluation for which the age was intuitively feeling, gave this search for liberation cogent expression in a new philosophy. Disturbed by various restrictive factors in the Russian state, by the significant suicide of Mayakovsky, and by the deaths of Yessenin and Bagnitsky; and facing up to the sinister influences apparent in such occurrences as the Moscow treason trial, with others he found that he could no longer resist the conclusion that Marxism, like the other doctrinaire totalitarianisms, was structurally destructive of those very values which it always professed to maintain; and offered no liberty to the artist, no freedom for the efflorescence of the spirit. Basing its premises upon the intrinsic rights of the individual, anarchism lashed out at all forms of totalitarianism, Left or Right, that placed any restrictions upon the freedom of the human personaity.

In this, unexpected and unusual reinforcement came from

a new movement which had for several years[1] been flourishing in France and which now—largely through Herbert Read's instrumentality—began to be potent in English literary circles —Surrealism.[2] By its use of the newly realized realms of the unconscious and subconscious explored by Freud and the Austrian psycho-analysts, this movement developed a technique of automatism, of hallucinatory visions, of strangely moving imagery and symbolism which opened up new and fruitful possibilities. At the hands of its first protagonists, the poets André Breton, Paul Eluard, Tristan Tzara, and Louis Aragon, and the artists Arp, Miro, Chirico, Picasso, and Ernst, Surrealism had been used as a frequent weapon of political satire, and had joined forces with Marxism.[3] But in its most important manifestations now, in its fusion with the anarchism of Herbert Read, it was to lead to a new school that was quick to seize upon the constructive force of these new possibilities. In 1937 the Apocalypse[4] came into being, led by Henry Treece, J. F. Hendry, and G. S. Fraser. Among its aims (consistently with the objectives we have seen) it proposed a positive use of myth for the reintegration of human personality —where Surrealism had been negative; and (as was natural) a fuller liberation of man 'from the Machine Age and from mechanistic thinking'—where Surrealism had been Marxist.

It was an inevitable development from anarchism, and an organic attempt to satisfy deeply felt needs. It is well to note here the remarkable achievements which characterize this phase—particularly Henry Treece's *Ballad of the Prince*, and J. F. Hendry's *The Orchestral Mountain*, both of which in power of sustained imagery and rich lyrical vision bear comparison with any verse written in the last decade. We might also bear in mind that the works of Dylan Thomas and George

---

[1] *Manifesto of Surrealism*, ed. André Breton (1924); *Second Manifesto of Surrealism* (1929).

[2] The name came from a poem of Guillaume Apollinaire who was regarded by the Surrealists as one of their forerunners.

[3] The names of the surrealist periodicals are significant: *La Révolution Surréaliste*; *La Surréalisme au service de la révolution*.

[4] *The New Apocalypse* (Fortune Press, 1939); *The White Horseman* (Routledge, 1941).

Barker—two dominating figures who stand rather apart from the movement—also exercised a very strong formative influence. And so did Rilke whose tremendous powers had enabled him to achieve a poetic integration of his personality in face of all his fear of death; he was more fully appreciated by the Apocalyptics even than he had been by the Auden–Spender group.

To what extent then, it might be asked, has Apocalypticism, seeing its mode of growth and development, in its fuller amplification in the personalist philosophy, achieved its aim of the liberation of the spirit of man, and prepared the way for it by its principles?

The movement was guided throughout, as we have seen, by an instinctive aspiration; and fortunately the Apocalypse in its literary expression was enriched by the mysticism and the lyrical fervour of the Celtic temperament which obscured some of its inherent defects. Many serious deficiencies, however, marred and fettered its attempt to provide a fullness and comprehensiveness of philosophy—defects implicit in the bases of Read's anarchism. In Read's works one perceives that having cleared the ground for greater freedom—ideally his political philosophy was a kind of anarcho-syndicalism (and as an aesthete he made the fatal mistake of attempting, in effect, to identify his own area of consciousness with the whole of reality)—his philosophy, when it comes to the realm of the personal, and to the reality of the spiritual life itself, is halting and undeveloped; one comes upon a vacuum of reticences. He is oblivious, for instance, of the true relevance of the Christian verities; he shares the Apocalyptics' unsoundness in spiritual theology and Christology; and even upon such a major point as belief in personal immortality he is (as J. F. Hendry notices[1]) negative and ambiguous. And we find him saying significantly: 'I cannot conceive religion as anything but the expression of individual emotions.'[2] His chapter on 'The Importance of

[1] In a symposium of essays edited by Henry Treece upon *Herbert Read, an introduction to his work* (1944).
[2] In *Poetry and Anarchism*, p. 122.

Living' in that book is a revelation of his limitations. In short, *one finds that he has been thinking all along in the same terms, and in the same thought-forms, as those whom he most opposed.* Basically, therefore, here is an anthropocentric philosophy which has all the traditional defects of humanism— limitations which the Apocalyptics and the Personalists share and are as yet unable to transcend—in spite of their increasing interest in Berdyaev and Maritain. Stefan Schimanski is able to write: 'This faith in Man alone gives meaning and dignity to the individual person. . . . His ultimate freedom lies in his power to transfigure *within himself* the given situation'[1] (Schimanski's italics).

Alex Comfort in an otherwise magnificent poem is able to say:[2]

> *I have been raised again*
> *out of the dead-cart, the corpse-pit of Citizens*
> *not by Christ but by Poetry . . .*

where an adequate Christology would not permit him for a moment to make use of such words in an empty symbolism. Without a completer grasp of Christian theology and sociology —not to mention soteriology—these dangers, one finds, of verse being unconsciously marred in this way by unrecognized implications are everywhere present throughout the movement.

It is thus difficult to see how modern Anarchism and Personalism can avoid the kind of fate which Read himself defines in these words: 'The truth is that modern man can never escape from himself. He carries his warped psychology about with him no less inevitably than his bodily diseases. But the worst disease is the one he creates out of his own isolation: uncritical phantasies, personal symbols, private fetishes . . .'[3] We see humanism, that anthropocentric standard which bases the rights of man upon a mere *ipse dixit*, standing in this movement upon the slippery slopes of relativism. Read has no

[1] In *Transformation*, III, 13.   [2] *The Song of Lazarus* (1945).
[3] *Poetry and Anarchism*, p. 19.

reply, save this—'a realistic rationalism'; 'a realistic rational-ism rises above all these diseases of the spirit'.[1] Apart from the lively retort which questions how such rationalism can be reconciled with the concept of unreason as used by the sur-realists, Berdyaev's analysis of rationalism (as being only one step removed from materialism) might here be pondered over.[2]

The Apocalypse too has only a refinement of that answer of Read's; and until Personalism in its various forms is able to break through this barrier into the liberation of a theocentric vision—which sees man's rights absolutely based upon his creation in God's image—this deficiency is likely to persist; and the new outlook will lack in the perception of the nature of spiritual reality; and literature will await either within or beyond Personalism a new revaluation and reorientation for which we can already discern the first intuitive stirrings.

[1] *Poetry and Anarchism*, p. 96.
[2] Nicolas Berdyaev, *Freedom and the Spirit*, p. 63 et seq.

PARTICULAR ESSAYS
ON ROMANTICISM IN MODERN
POETRY, THE CINEMA
AND
THE NOVEL

FRANCIS SCARFE

ROMANTICISM IN MODERN POETRY

I

IT is impossible to talk about Romanticism and Classicism long without talking nonsense. There is no satisfactory definition of either, save by their respective extremist partisans, and it is not the aim of this essay to arrive at a further definition. The French, who take a more pedantic interest than we do in such matters, have little compunction in saying that although Baudelaire was a Romantic, he was also 'classique par la forme'. The bogyman of Form is of course a Romantic ailment, witness the fate of Gautier, for whom it was merely a corrective to the triviality of his thought. Stylization usually occurs in societies in which the artist is the tool of tyranny, and the freedom with which artists contrive to work within the limits of such stylization shows that there is no formula capable of quenching the creative spirit of a true artist. It is possible that in a society such as ours, in which the artist's scope is unlimited, there is less real liberty, in the sense that we are reduced to the dull monotony of sensationalism and minor difference.

For the sake of argument, however, I advance two conceptions which may be of some value. The first is that Baudelaire defined Romanticism as 'une manière de sentir'—a way of feeling. Let us translate this into the usual hectic modern idiom and say, a crisis of feeling. It enables us to differentiate between Gray's *Elegy* and Pope's *Essay on Man*, for in the first the natural order is questioned and in the second it is accepted and even praised. Romanticism questions, Classicism knows all the answers. The second proposal is Mallarmé's, who said in an interview with Jules Huret that in modern society no synthesis, and therefore no Classicism, is possible, and he went on to say that the artist is thus forced into a position where he is occupied with hewing his own tomb. Lack of synthesis and enforced individualism; the poet's writing for numerous audiences from the mandarin to the factory hand, for the right, left and centre, for the agnostic and unbeliever, and the Peculiar People, and in the last resort for himself. Writing in the era of ATOBOMB SLAYS CITY headlines, where the bust no longer survives the city and the poem is as ephemeral as yesterday's *Daily Mail* or the stock exchange ticker.

Mallarmé suggests that in a society where there is an established hierarchy and where the same political and religious views are held by a community, Classicism may be achieved. The professorial historians of literature need to revise their books. They have told us for so long that Classicism was achieved, for instance, in seventeenth-century France (and indeed we come nearest to it in modern times under benevolent and not so benevolent despots). This can only be argued by closing one eye to that stream of poetry which, beginning with Scève and passing through the Pléiade, Saint-Amant and Théophile, produced that wonderful river of Baroque poetry which has not yet been fully explored, and with which the nineteenth-century Symbolists had so much in common. But it is interesting to note a possible implication of Mallarmé's statement, which is that 'classicism' or a synthesis of some kind will some day be produced in the ordered states of Soviet Russia or Socialist Britain, and we will all live happily ever after.

The term 'Romanticism' is a comparatively modern one, and if it is to be used at all I would prefer it to be used historically. The age of poetry in which we are living is to all intents and purposes the age inaugurated by Blake and Wordsworth. Symbolism and Surrealism are two of its tributaries. If we accept a purely historical use of the term, then obviously one cannot write about 'Romanticism in Modern Poetry', though it might be possible to say a few words about certain aspects of modern poetry which bear out such an historical interpretation.

II

Reporting and interpretation have been two obvious characteristics of poetry in recent years, partly because the inter-war years raised problems of the dignity of man which the poet could not ignore, and partly because in wartime the conditions of life are so exotic and tragic that the poet cannot escape describing and mourning over them. Much of the poetry of this type can be dismissed as minor poetry, indeed sometimes not poetry at all. By reporting, I mean descriptions of life in which the poet is an observer only, and we must exempt those works in which the poet describes something of which he is a part. For instance the battlefield poems of Keith Douglas are acceptable because he described something in which he was actively and not merely sympathetically involved. Some poems which are often hastily classed as 'reporting' are much more than that, and in such poems as Auden's 'Spain', Barker's elegy on the same theme, the subject is treated imaginatively and with the full range of an artist's knowledge of his craft. I have always felt that Day Lewis's poem about the air-trip to Australia by Macintosh failed in this respect, for it was more descriptive than imaginative. This of course raises further problems, and it is necessary to define participation as more than physical presence, but emotional and imaginative presence. Of the actual 'reporting' poetry, however, for instance much of what appeared in the anthology of poems for Spain, and what has appeared in war-anthologies more recently, the poverty of the means discredits most of it in advance. It is enough to say that while the social-content question is far from dead, in certain aspects of their work modern poets have come closer to the newspaper and the *fait-divers* than is desirable. There is no need to rehearse the minute particularities of the Kippsian outlook which our poets have visited upon us. Time has proved that their outbursts were necessary, but those once exciting topical volumes are now sadly closed; they demonstrate how fatal it is to be always right. In spite of this, however, we must acknowledge that such poetry has come to stay: it is of the variety which Baudelaire himself praised in Pierre Dupont, it is as necessary as bread. Poets, however, are usually expected to make cake. The point I would leave here is that there are certain poets whose task it is to make the Crown Jewels. It may be that these makers of Crown Jewels are the Classicists of each age: not so long ago we had Valéry and Rilke. These are not poets for the masses, however broad and humane their outlook was, however necessary it may be for the public, through minor channels, to absorb gradually their outlook and their magnificence. As the Crown Jewels are a recognized and necessary symbol of royalty and power, so certain poems are the outward symbol of poetry itself, of the divine muse which is both sacred and magic. And even at the present time we have one or two such makers, patiently working on something unbelievably rare and useless and beautiful, which the crowd will never quite comprehend but to which it will bow down in reverence and homage. Such poets must be mystics, whether of the Rosy Cross or of the Hegelian dialectic, and they must have a high purpose to make art out of a stone, or to hew poems out of intractable material as Eliot is now doing. To return to Mallarmé for a moment, in hewing his own tomb the poet may also be erecting the monument of a civilization.

Let us return for the moment from the makers of the Crown Jewels to the common journeyman of poetry, more concerned with goods for daily consumption by rich and poor alike, but above all for those who will take them here and now. Even these humble poets, who are in a vast majority, have a mighty task before them. Living in this romantic age, the modern poet has to invent his own symbols and terms of reference, symbols which will be understood by the Peculiar People and the Jehovah's Witness alike. The mythology of Greece and Rome, which fortunately Giraudoux and Cocteau are trying to rejuvenate, is now little more than a fairy tale, a reassuring bedtime story which the Heath-Stubbses (and I say this with some respect, for there is a good artist up the wrong street, trying to get back to the womb in the traditional public-school manner) use as a decorative motif for not always so reassuring poems.

It would be foolish to criticize classical mythology itself; I am merely attacking its constant misuse by generations of mediocre Georgians and pedants. If we are to use it vitally, it must be through a reinterpretation in the light of our own experience, and that reinterpretation can produce a living poetry only in the light of modern psychological theory and anthropology. The real fault is that there are so few poets capable of using that mythology without falling into sentimental bewilderment. Yeats and Eliot have used it sparingly and with success, and only Pound and Joyce have integrated it into their work without being completely overwhelmed.

Unless myth is a part of our daily lives it will produce no more than a barren echo in poetry. The reason is usually that the associated imagery is restricted. 'The mission of art is to represent, in sensible forms, the free development of life and above all of the spirit.' I know of no better definition of the purpose of art than that of Hegel, and the development of life implies a development of mythology and of the forms of the imagination. There is hardly a step between the outlook of the greatest of the Romantic philosophers and the great Romantic artist, Delacroix, for whom 'The world is a vast dictionary which only the artist can decipher'.

The younger poets have undertaken, consciously, this task of deciphering the world, and above all the inner world of the spirit, and for this they need more than an overworked mythology. Blake was the first poet in modern Europe to realize the need for new terms of reference, and his implications were more than Platonic when he exclaimed, 'One power alone makes a poet: Imagination, the Divine Vision'. Our poetry today is nearer in every respect to the Imagination of Blake than to that of Coleridge or Wordsworth. Symbolism and Surrealism have intervened but only to confirm Blake's greatness, and to give us a language better equipped for the task he set poetry. Language needed enlarging, especially after the concept of the unconscious and subconscious mind was clearly formulated and backed by practical experiment, and the poets were faced with the problem of giving expression to images and sensations, dreams and visions which, long submerged through centuries of taboo, laid a heavier burden on our habits of thought and language than they had previously been expected to bear.

The result is that, Romantic or not, modern poetry is a poetry of liberated imagination. The imagery of the twentieth century is or should be an imagery divested of sin. A language also divested of sin, as Joyce and Henry Miller have proved. All forms, words, and substances are established in their own right. We see this innocence daily in the work of such poets as Thomas and Barker, where language and imagery are purified and enriched in a great reconciliation with life.

At the same time the paws of doctrine still hold the poet down. The expansion of language has moved faster than is fully realized, and the new-found freedom has not always been wisely enjoyed. Craftsmanship has been altogether discarded in the blind pursuit of our new understanding of man and his speech. Every revolution needs to be consolidated: the twentieth-century revolution in poetry is still in its period of chaos and experiment. To quote Hegel again: 'Language for the poet is only a means of external transmission, and a pure sign with which his thought is not confused.' Much unsuccessful poetry is being written now not only because of the vanity of those who are unwilling to learn the first principles of its craft, but above all because language is being regarded as an end in itself. Sensitiveness to language avails little unless there is sensitiveness to experience, and experience itself is of no worth to a poet unless it is to some degree organized and integrated. Whatever the extent to which a poet can liberate himself, he should never forget Arnold's warning that 'For poetry the idea is everything'.

The mythologies with which the modern poet is naturally concerned, since the development of social and psychological knowledge, are chiefly related to the ideologies of societies now hardening into set patterns such as Communism and Democracy, and secondly, the place of the individual in such societies, particularly in view of the findings of psycho-analysis. In both of those fields Blake was a pioneer: he had to a unique degree what may be called social imagination, and on the other hand there is some truth in Middleton Murry's assertion that Blake was 'the father of modern psychology'. No poet since Blake has been able to achieve such a synthesis between the social and psychological, because none has been capable of creating his own symbols and his own techniques.

The sociological myth has failed, and we have not proceeded beyond the romantic perception of a world in ruins, portrayed by such poems as 'The Waste Land' or Jules Romains's 'L'Homme blanc'. I doubt whether our democracy will ever find its true poet. D. H. Lawrence, after Whitman, came near at least to a perception of the need, but was too spontaneous and impatient to build—like Burns, he expressed his social attitudes in an enduring lyrical form, but failed when it came to the architecture of a great work. The modern poets certainly seem to be incapable of building; perhaps we have reached the stage where a great collective poem, like the Iliad, is awaited.

Our most successful modern poetry has been related to the development of psychology as a science. Mallarmé's 'Après-midi d'un Faune' in the late nineteenth century established the archetype of introspective poem—and it is now a myth as established as those of Greece. Valéry's 'La Jeune Pàrque', Tzara's 'L'Homme approximatif', and some of the work of Eliot and Thomas are in the same line. Browning's use of the dramatic monologue was prophetic: it certainly influenced Mallarmé, Valéry, and Eliot, but our young poets only dimly realize its implications—they are too impatient to follow anything but their own primitive urge. To that extent they cease to be poets, but in the wider sense they are *novateurs*, for the exploration of the deeper levels of mind and the development of language to meet it, with all its new range of symbols, is probably as much as can be expected of any one generation of poets. This is no age of masterpieces; it is an age of exploration.

STEPHEN WATTS

ROMANTICISM IN THE CINEMA

SOME days after I had received from the publisher the few
copies of a novel of mine which an author may now have
without the penalty of feeling he is paying his own royalties, I noticed that on the spine of the jacket were printed
words I had previously overlooked. They read 'An unusual
and attractive romance' and my immediate reaction was
annoyance. On further thought, however, this annoyance
shrank while another grew in its place. Originally, the words
offended because taken together they made up an advertising
phrase or label which might equally well have been applied to
the work of Mesdames Denise Robins or Berta Ruck and my
snobbish instinct was to resent the association. But take the
phrase apart. It would be ungracious to resent either of the
adjectives. What then was my complaint, or in the language
to which I am daily exposed in the cinema, what was I beefing
about? It must lie in the word 'romance'. But objection there
could only be on the ground of the secondary, vulgar or
degraded definition of what is otherwise a fine, pedigreed,
even noble word. Alas, not for romance itself but for its decline
and fall in popular usage! I was annoyed with myself for
joining, by implication and instinct, the big battalions of near-
illiteracy.

Even more in the world of fiction films than in that of fiction
books—I choose my words to make it clear that at this stage I
am not discussing art and literature—romance means simply
love-story. And the corrupt simplification goes further. Love-
story means a more or less rigid formula which is often referred
to briefly by weary critics as 'boy-meets-girl'. I have noticed
that this phrase is often misunderstood. It is merely an easy
reference, not a full description. It does not mean just what

it says, as people I have heard use it seem to imagine. The rest of the formula is '. . . boy loses girl, boy gets girl'. It is that formal pattern of encounter, misunderstanding, and reconciliation which constitutes the convention criticized. It is that formula, and not just the first of its three components, which film producers apparently have labelled, boldly and untransferably, in their card-indexes of plots. 'Romance' the label reads, in block capitals, probably neon-lit and in gorgeous Technicolor. It is that label one has to tear out and tear up before one can discuss the romantic element in films with any reasonable hope of being understood by readers whose minds are still substantially uncorrupted and unenslaved to Hollywood dictation as to the meaning of good words gone wrong.

Another prerequisite is to establish what romance does and can mean *in the cinema* as distinct from its wider applications in art. This can be done most quickly, and with workmanlike if not ideal exactitude, by antonyms. If the opposite of the romantic in art-at-large is the classical, the opposite of the romantic in the cinema is the realistic, there being no such thing as the classical film. Another way of putting it: the infusion into the narrative chronicle of contributions by the imagination and of elements which recognize the supernatural are the distinguishing features of romantic story-telling; this applies to story-telling by means of cinematography, with the extension that the medium, being not words alone but light and shade and visual movement and the manipulation of animate and inanimate bodies, is amenable to far more elastic interpretations of such elements.

Enough of definitions, though they are necessary in clearing the ground. There is no room for applying in the cinema Goethe's dubious maxim: 'Classicism is health; Romanticism is disease', for, as I have said, there is no cinematic classicism. But bending the epigram unscrupulously to my purpose I would give as a text for what follows my capsulated belief that in films unremitting realism is death; romanticism is life, or at least a useful form of artificial respiration.

Although the range of reference in the cinema is limited to

a mere half-century or so, access to work in existence is infinitely more difficult than in the realm of literature. There can be, I imagine, relatively few people whose film-watching goes far enough back for them to be wondering as they read why I have not yet cited the great romantic piece of the old cinema by pointing to the dusty corner of the museum where the *Nibelungen Lied* lies mouldering. It is indeed a museum piece. I was entranced by the film when I saw it some fifteen years ago, largely because I had never seen anything remotely like it in the cinema before. Nor can I recall anything like it since. Whatever it started in cinema, it finished too.

But through the agency of film societies it has been possible to see in my adult lifetime a sufficient representation of what has been done or attempted on the screen to be able to gauge the temper, the fashions, the evolution as well as the individual achievements of the film's childhood and adolescence, if indeed that latter, febrile period may yet be said to have passed.

The movement, broadly, has been from the romantic towards the realistic, with attractive excursions along the side-lanes of fantasy. It is not my purpose nor that of this book to attempt even an abridged history of films or to rehearse a catalogue of titles. The significant thing about the 'movement' I have mentioned is that the people who have taken part in it at the top, the executives and producers employing the artists, i.e. the directors and writers and players, have either been quite unaware of it or have, in my opinion, misinterpreted it. They have seen it, in most cases, simply as 'progress'. Always vocal in their determination to 'give the public what it wants' they are in a position only to check the public response to what they have given. And what they have given has owed its form, its changes and revolutions, to the men they have employed, the artists. I believe that the artists, if we leave out the players this time, are fully aware of the undulating graph-like nature of film history in terms of content. They do not see it as the straight line of development, such as might be pursued by a motor-car factory. But to the executive in the front office a studio is rather like a motor-car factory. Get the best-selling model on the road at the lowest cost consistent with the profit it is intended to make. The fact that movies are made out of an intractable and unbudgetable substance called ideas must, when they think of it, be a source of maddening irritation to them.

I want to get the executives and the big-money men out of the way quickly. They have little positive connection with what goes on the screen, though in some cases they exercise a pernicious negative influence. The film, in the commercial studio, tends to be as good as the Big Boss will permit it to be. He is not 'in films' to express himself or to put his creations proudly before the public. He is working for the stockholders. It is sometimes important to remember this, because the realization will at times make sense—and at other times beautiful nonsense—of the pronouncements of film-business men who tend to pursue a course of self-delusion that they are (a) artists, (b) objective critics, (c) humble servants of the public, and (d) high-minded philanthropists.

It has become almost trite to say that David Wark Griffith was the father and pioneer of the fiction film as we know it. But the point germane to our subject here is that in terms of the spirit and content and manner of the photoplay ('sun-play' was the extraordinarily prehistoric-sounding title Griffith first used) his heyday saw the infant cinema through a condition of flux. At that time it is just to say that the whole artistic future of the film was in Griffith's hands; his problems were the root problems of story-telling by camera, his experiments were the whole research laboratory of a potential art-form. Griffith, a passionate and sincere artist, was after a dozen things at once. He hankered after the classical. He was of himself a romantic and a sentimentalist. He was also a stern, somewhat naïve, moralist. He was a restless, questing experimentalist. He loved spectacle, the drama of big dimensions; sometimes, watching his work, you wonder if he was trying to discover if there were *any* limits to the sheer size of the story the screen could carry, to the complexities of counterpoint and cutting which could heighten the emotional effect of the visual narrative. Griffith at the height of his career was the labouring womb of whatever art there is in the film.

From this welter of experimentation in which inspiration and crudity, originality, and convention mingled uneasily, the film emerged on to the relatively smooth path of technical competence. What was to be said was subjugated to how it should be said. The legs which ideas are said to have seemed to develop rickets while technique grew firm-boned into a sturdy, cocksure brat and raced off almost out of sight.

(A parenthesis here: I have been dealing with the 'straight' story, but it would put the picture out of focus if I did not make a marginal note on comedy. In this *genre* Chaplin was as original, as inventive as, and perhaps even more ingenious than Griffith. In his early films, as most readers will recall, his was an almost purely romantic vein. The chronicles of the tramp were no faithful documents. Fancy and caprice informed every other sequence. The glimpse of the huddled steerage passengers in *The Immigrant* almost shocked me when I saw it recently in the thirtieth year of its age. The satire on the arrivals in 'the land of freedom' held back by ropes, corralled and abused by officialdom, was a surprising pleasure, because these were not the things for which one remembered Chaplin. But comedy is another pasture, into which I dare not wander in this article.)

When the way of the technically expert film had become smooth, with most of the mechanical and processing problems solved, interest in the film's content seems to have risen again. But convention's heavy hand still detained the creative mind and spirit. Boy was in the saddle, girl on the pommel (except during the misunderstanding section when she was in the beleaguered and/or mortgaged cabin, awaiting rescue) and romance in its debased meaning was as firmly imbedded as the stars' footprints in the concrete outside Grauman's Chinese Theatre, tourist showplace of Hollywood, Cal., Mecca of the movie world, shrine of the subnormal.

It would, of course, be possible to make a list of films containing genuinely romantic elements which were made in, say, the ten years before the outbreak of war in 1939. It would look impressive only so long as no account was taken of the aggregate number of films made in the period, which would run most of the way into five figures. Of these the overwhelming majority could be categorized as conventionally 'romantic' with an increasing realism in the rendering of the romance.[1] Realism *manqué*. Realism only so long as it was amenable to having the untidy ends tucked safely into the 'romantic' perambulator.

Now it may be argued that most of the period in the decade before World War II was so distressful in world affairs that from 1931 onwards it was so clearly a rumbling prelude to war that the film-makers, always sensitive to 'topicality', must naturally have been impelled to realism. It is a superficially impressive argument, dubious if considered further, for the film-makers have always tended to romanticize the real, just as they have held down the truly romantic elements by the determination to make the resulting production 'realistic'. Thus if topicality pushed them towards 'real' themes their own conventions and their convictions about public taste sugared most of the genuine reality out of the finished films. No, the increasing realism of films was, I am sure, due principally to the increasing ability of the studios to be realistic. It is probably natural to do most, to prefer to do, what one does best. Set-building (so confusingly known as 'art direction') was now an advanced craft. Photography and the cutting or editing of the sets of photographs—perhaps the great single factor influencing the effect produced by the impact of a film on the mind and senses of the spectator—had reached high levels of

[1] I do not mean there had been any conscious choice of 'realism' or any other explicit and recognized form or style and a rejection of romanticism. It was all much simpler and less self-conscious than that. Alistair Cooke wrote some years ago as good a one-sentence explanation of the average producer's intentions as I have read: 'The producers knew the sort of audience they had to cater for and they worked logically and exactly to use a type of entertainment which would play on simple sensation and not disturb the audience with literary irrelevances like imagination, verisimilitude, subtle characterization.' He was writing of the very early days. Later physical verisimilitude became almost a passion. The rest stands.

proficiency, and even artistry. The style of acting favoured was an extreme of lifelike naturalism where the highest tribute an actor could be paid was, 'Why, he didn't seem to be acting at all!' Skill was abundant, though in application it often degenerated into slickness; imagination and ideas, always in short supply, were at a discount.

There was another cause of the pursuit of realism. The books and plays gaining widest notice in the period were in the main realistic in style, or sentimental-realistic would perhaps be a better description. And the cinema draws most of its plot-material from books and plays. This produces, especially in America, a circle, vicious or merely venal, because novelists and playwrights tend to write with an eye on Hollywood, for the sale of the screen rights brings them vastly more money than the royalties on the best of best-sellers or the longest stage runs. So the sentimental-realistic was the film fashion, though to complete another of those tiresome circles, it was commonly known by the name properly belonging to that style and spirit it most specifically rejected, for these were the 'romances' of the screen, this was the cinema at the height of its 'romantic' form. It had never been less truly romantic.

As I am dealing with the bulk-product of the cinema I cannot extend my survey as far as I would wish into the field of foreign-language films because in proportion their volume was and is negligible, though their interest is great. The French were producing a characteristically varied bag. There was romanticism in Clair, realism in Renoir, a different romanticism in much of Feyder, and so on. The Russians were set in their course of realism, but a realism which was actuality itself compared with Hollywood's. When their purposes of propaganda, domestic or external, inflated their mood to the heroic it was never romantic in essence; they seemed to be saying, with a heavy seriousness and great technical resource: 'This is precisely what happened, and our first purpose is to convince you that it did happen, to move you to pride in the achievement and bind you in sympathy and loyalty to the people who did or are doing such things.' Germany, having made the earliest truly romantic films, had only a few years to live, artistically, in the period under review before the darkness of 1933 settled on their studios. The German contribution became merged with the American, and with the British to a less extent with the exodus of their studios' best brains. The Fritz Lang who made the strange, clumsy but exciting *Destiny* became the Fritz Lang who made the brilliantly realistic *Fury*, and then turned to the 'psychological thriller' never to return—or at least I shall be very surprised if he returns now—to the high romantic mood which he obviously first conceived as that in which he could best develop as an artist of the cinema.

Let me round off this pre-war period with one indicative anecdote. A very beautiful film was made of Maxwell Anderson's poetic play, *Winterset*. The basic story of this play might have been told in terms of quite ordinary melodrama. But someone, greatly daring, not only retained Mr. Anderson's blank verse and ensured its very beautiful speaking by engaging a fine stage actor, Burgess Meredith, to play the main part, but also conceived a setting and a style for the screen version which ensured that its romantic qualities would be heightened and intensified rather than dissipated in the cinema. To a film critic, habitually braced to receive the average die-stamp film drama, this picture came as a glorious shock. Still a little dazed by the beauty, the artistic integrity and bold refusal to compromise that I had witnessed, I walked out of the first London showing and met a well-known film producer. 'Wonderful,' he murmured in my ear. 'Wonderful. I'd hate to have a penny in it.'

The years I have been discussing did, of course, produce some romantic films apart from *Winterset*, but there was nothing arising from them that could be analysed as a trend. They each of them existed in splendid isolation. Some were not wholly romantic or consistently so, but contained recognizable romantic elements. In British there were *Fire Over England* and *Tudor Rose*, the latter a small-scale triumph for its writer-director, Robert Stevenson, who had a low budget and much opposition and yet gave the picture the mixture of intimacy and spaciousness, the romantic flourish, for which he earnestly strove. From France there came *La Kermesse hero-ïque* and the exquisite *Mayerling*. From Hollywood I recall more particularly two films which were romantically conceived but became bogged down in what for brevity I shall merely call Hollywoodism. There was *Camille,* in which Greta Garbo gave ample evidence of her superlative ability (well known already to the relatively few who had seen her, aged seventeen, in the Swedish *Gösta Berling*)[1] to encompass the romantic mood and style if only her associates would sustain it and her; and there was *Lost Horizon*, which missed its high target (though remaining a far more than averagely interesting film) because its creators, Frank Capra and his writer, Robert Riskin, brought to their task what had been a masterly equip- ment in previous films but was out of place here—a sympa- thetic deftness in the rendering of the comedy-sentimentalism of ordinary people in odd situations. A director with a flair for romanticism might have made *Lost Horizon* memorable.

Contrary to a popular belief that film fashions change every other day and film personalities last only a few years, change comes slowly in pictures. (On the second of these popular beliefs it is only necessary to say that most of the important people engaged in film-making have been at it for about twenty years and a good proportion of the principal players have at least ten years of stardom behind them.) It is necessary therefore to go back a few years at least to see if there can be

---

[1] Writing of this early Garbo film recently, Dilys Powell made this excellent comment on romanticism in films then and now. I quote with her permission: '. . . the Gösta Berling of the film is the hero of the nineteenth-century romantic age, compassing within himself the extremes of suffering and happiness, self-sacrifice and self-indulgence. It is this violent romantic approach which the cinema has lost nowadays. Stiller in *The Atonement of Gösta Berling*, Griffith in *Intolerance*, in their several ways felt evil as something tangible—and something gigantic. The contemporary cinema has dwarfed evil. In this, of course, it is not alone; for the modern tendency is to reject the old notion of excess, whether of good or bad. (One might add that the experiences of the past decade have, by their very size, deadened sensibility to evil.) But of the cinema in particular it might be said that an attention to the wrong kind of realism is partly to blame.
'The film is a realistic medium; nobody can say that the settings of Stiller's work are not realistic. But it is also, or should be, a poetic medium: apt to poetry in its interpretation of character and its rendering of mood.'

detected any trend which shows signs of consistent, or even sporadic, development, which gives evidence of being more than a fad, fashion, or aspect of some real or imagined topicality. For this purpose I have drawn up a list of the outstanding pictures of the war years. Now these were not by any means all made under the stresses and influences of war. The films of 1940, for example, were mostly made before even Europe's, far less America's, war had begun. There is not a trace of a war subject among them. There were two notable excursions into the fantastic, *The Wizard of Oz* and Disney's charming *Pinocchio*. There were two much-publicized novelettes—*Gone with the Wind* and *Rebecca*. There was a glorious Lubitsch–Garbo comedy, *Ninotchka*. There was the profoundly real and moving *Grapes of Wrath*. There was a return by Gary Cooper to his best manner in a spirited and sensible Western called *The Westerner*. There was the Cronin chronicle of coal and milk-pudding politics, *The Stars Look Down*, given more than its merits in terms of artistic film-making by Carol Reed. There was a juicy slice of charm in *Pride and Prejudice* and a complete absence of Jane's astringent sauce. There was an unusual piece, verging on whimsy but saved by simple sincerity, called *Our Town*, from Thornton Wilder's play. And there was Chaplin's robust and delightful comment on a world reeling downhill to God-knew-what—*The Great Dictator*. You will observe that cataloguing achieves nothing. Or if you can argue anything from that heterogeneous group you are a better arguer and a far more percipient analyst than I can claim to be.

But wait—what does 1941 show? Do we begin to get somewhere? *The Long Voyage Home. Love on the Dole. Pimpernel Smith. Lady Hamilton. Citizen Kane. Sullivan's Travels.* Short of giving a synopsis of these pictures, with notes on how they were handled on the screen, I cannot demonstrate, step by persuasive step, how they seem to evince a hint, a glimmer, a whisper, of—what? In my opinion, there is evidence of a slight extension in the conception of the film-story, a raising of the imaginative level, a swelling of the seed of . . . but my eye has just wandered on to 1942 and I find little to support my too hastily detected trend. My heart sinks as I survey the staginess of *The Little Foxes*, the good, old-fashioned tough slickness of *Roxie Hart* (most enjoyable but proving nothing), the beautiful mindlessness of *Blood and Sand*. And the war films are with us now; good ones, I admit, like *One of our Air-craft is Missing, In which We Serve* and *The First of the Few*. Then I come to *Mrs. Miniver,* one of the great box-office successes of our time and just about as near as the cinema has ever come to acting on me as an emetic.

Still, one example to cheer me peeps out shyly from between *Yankee Doodle Dandy* and *George Washington Slept Here*. It is *Thunder Rock*, a bravely supernatural piece. I beg leave to let it serve as the needed link as we pass to 1943.

But my courage is oozing away. Mere chapter and verse, examples seized from a context riddled with contradictions and chanciness, will not make a case. Let me simply evoke memories with odd names. *The Magnificent Ambersons. The Seventh Cross. For Whom the Bell Tolls* with a rather large question mark after it. *Henry V*.[1]

Where do we go from here? Looking at the titles I have cited I wonder if there is any genuine common element, any real string upon which to thread these real and cultured pearls of such wildly varied size, colour, and quality. I turn to my encyclopaedia for light in my gathering gloom and find the great Saintsbury writing:

'. . . Romance on the whole and with some flashes of better things at times is a jumble of incoherent and mostly ill-told stories, combining sameness with extravagance, outraging probability and the laws of imitative form, childish as a rule in its appeal to adventure and to the supernatural, immoral in its ethics, barbarous in its aesthetics, destitute of any philo-

---

[1] A relevant but ironic comment is that during the war there was made in France a perfect example of the bad romantic film, Cocteau's *L'Eternel Retour*, heavily Germanic in style, Nazified in its treatment of the Tristan story, beautiful at moments in its ponderous way but deplorable in its sickly idealization of fates and destinies, inexorable, amoral, capable of fulfilling the dreams of the intellectually debased.

sophy, representing at its very best a necessary stage in the education of half-civilised peoples. . . .'

So far, it might be the story of the cinema by one of its harsher critics! Then:

'On the other hand, for the last hundred years and more there have been some who have seen in romance almost the highest and certainly the most charming form of fictitious creation, the literary embodiment of men's dreams and desires. . . .'

Now we are nearer what we seek. Briefly I believe that there is an increasing desire, by the better practising artists working in the medium of the film, to break down conventional walls, to paint their pictures in bolder colours, mixing more imaginative vigour and freedom with their pigments, and, for a third metaphor, casting aside the uniform garments of the inhibited 'commercial film' in favour of brighter, more fanciful costume. The identification of the spectator with the image-creature of the screen has long been an integral of the film's power. But the objects of identification have too long been dull, meretricious, and material. The embodiment of dreams and desires of which Saintsbury speaks can be in shapes which permit of the existence of the spirit of man as well as his lust for material advantage. The film always has sought to take us 'out of ourselves.' And it has very largely succeeded. But out of ourselves into what? Into mere envy, mere castle-building, with their ebb-tide of discontent and depression? The more successful the truly romantic experimenters in film fiction are, the more will the man in the one-and-threepennies be likely to experience that enlargement of himself which induces stimulus instead of self-pity. But I have no wish to push this argument into realms of 'uplift' which is no concern of art except in a very specialized sense. I don't want the seeker after relaxation in the cinema to see films which are going to 'do him good'. It will be enough if with a movement in films away from 'romance' towards romance the artistic dimensions of the cinema are extended and the flow of honest expression from the artist in the studio is made wider, stronger, and fresher.

HOW A ROMANTIC NOVEL WAS EVOLVED

INTRODUCTION

TITUS GROAN was begun in 1940, as a page of nonsensical conversation between two pompous half-wits, but this was quickly abandoned—indeed it was only written because there was pen and paper to hand. It led, however, to another couple of characters leaning against one another, back to back, in a high room before dawn. Descriptions of the room, the river below the window, and more conversation followed. A mixture of serious as well as nonsensical fantasy began to pour itself out, without object, sentences growing out of their precursors involuntarily. About three chapters were written like this and then scrapped when the idea of Gormenghast began to evolve. From then on I wrote intermittently, at short rapid intervals, never knowing a line ahead—far less a chapter. Most of it was composed in the Army 1940–43, at odd moments. Earlier chapters were changed in 1944, for the 'feel' of the book had become more serious—or at least the imagination grew darker—the comic moments farther and farther apart, and as the characters themselves and the story, per se, developed, something more important seemed to be materializing.

As I went along I made drawings from time to time which helped me to visualize the characters and to imagine what sort of things they would say. The drawings were never exactly as I imagined the people, but were near enough for me to know when their voices lost touch with their heads. What sense of incompletion there is at the end of the book (the main character being only eighteen months old) I have attempted to nullify by the symbolism of Titus's coming into his inherit-

STUDY FOR STEERPIKE

STUDY FOR FUCHSIA

Swelter
with Kitchen
urchin

STUDY FOR SWELTER WITH URCHIN

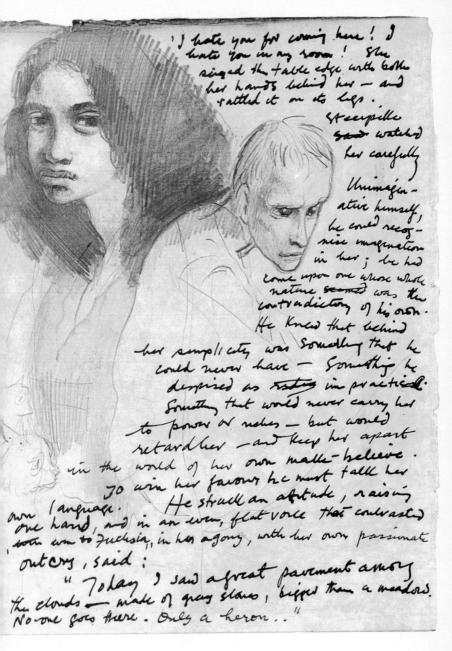

'I hate you for coming here! I hate you in my room!' She singed the table edge with both her hands behind her — and rattled it on its legs.

Steerpike said watched her carefully

Unimaginative himself, he could recognise imagination in her; he had come upon one whose whole nature seemed was the contradictory of his own. He knew that behind her simplicity was something that he could never have — something he despised as usless impractical. Something that would never carry her to power or riches — but would retard her — and keep her apart in the world of her own make-believe. To win her favour he must talk her own language. He struck an attitude, raising one hand, and in an even, flat voice that contrasted both even to Fuchsia, in her agony, with her own passionate outcry, said:

"Today I saw a great pavement among the clouds — made of grey stones, bigger than a meadow. No-one goes there. Only a heron..."

MANUSCRIPT PAGE
WITH SKETCHES OF FUCHSIA AND STEERPIKE

ance. I have tried to make the book artistically complete, although the story is obviously unfinished. I hope it will complete itself in the next book.

1

EMPTINESS OF GORMENGHAST

It was as though, at any moment, some inanimate Thing must surely move; a door open upon its own, or a clock start whirling its hands: the stillness was too vast and charged to be content to remain in this titanic atrophy—the tension must surely find a vent—and burst suddenly, violently, like a reservoir of water from a smashed dam—and the shields fall from their rusty hooks, the mirrors crack, the boards lift and open and the very castle tremble, shake its walls like wings; yawn, split and crumble with a roar.

But nothing happened. Each hall a mouth that gaped and could not close. The stone jaws prised and aching. The doors like eye-teeth missing from the bone! There was no sound and nothing human happened.

What moved in these great caves? A shifting shadow? Only where sunlight through the south wing wandered. What else? No other movement?

Only the deathly padding of the cats. Only the soundlessness of the dazed cats—the line of them—the undulating line as blanched as linen, and lorn as the long gesture of a hand.

Where, in the wastes of the forsaken castle, spellbound with stone lacunas—where could they find their way? From hush to hush. All was unrooted. Life, bone and breath; echo and movement gone. . . .

They flowed. Noiselessly and deliberately they flowed. Through doors ajar they flowed on little feet. The stream of them. The cats.

Under the welkin of the flaking cherubs doming through shade, they ran. The pillars narrowing in chill perspective formed them their mammoth highway. The refectory opened up its tracts of silence. Over the stones they ran. Along a corridor of fissured plaster. Room after hollow room—hall after hall, gallery after gallery, depth after depth, until the acres of grey kitchen opened. The chopping blocks, the ovens and grills, stood motionless as altars to the dead. Far below the warped beams they flowed in a white band. There was no hesitation in their drift. The tail of the white line had disappeared, and the kitchen was as barren as a cave in a lunar hillside. They were swarming up cold stairs to other lands.

Where has she gone? Through the drear sub-light of a thousand yawns, they ran, their eyes like moons. Up winding stairs to other worlds again, threading the noonday dusk. And they could find no pulse and she was gone.

Yet there was no cessation. League after league, the swift, unhurried padding. The pewter room slid by, the bronze room and the iron. The armoury slid by on either side—the passageways slid by—on either side—and they could find no breath in Gormenghast.

The doorway of the Hall of the Bright Carvings was ajar. As they slid through the opening it was as though a long, snow-soft serpent had appeared, its rippling body sewn with yellow eyes. Without a pause it streamed among the carvings lifting hundreds of little dust clouds from the floor. It reached the hammock at the shuttered end, where, like a continuation of silence and stillness in a physical form, dozed the curator, the only living thing in the castle apart from the feline snake that was flooding past him and was even now on its way back to the door. Above it, the coloured carvings smouldered. The golden mule—the storm-grey child—the wounded head with locks of chasmic purple.

2

STEERPIKE'S CLIMB UP THE IVY

As the light began to wane, twenty-four hours after he had lain above the prison room on the sloping roof of slates, he came to the foot of that high wall, near the summit of which was the window he had seen three hours previously. There he rested. He was about midway between the ground two hundred feet below him and the window. He had been accurate in his observation when he had guessed that the face of the wall was covered over its entire area with a thick, ancient growth of ivy. As he sat against the wall, his back against the enormous hairy stem of the creeper as thick as the bole of a tree, the ivy leaves hung far out and over him and, turning his head upwards, he found that he was gazing into a profound and dusty labyrinth. He knew that he would have to climb through darkness, so thick was the skein of the coarse, monotonous foliage; but the limbs of the straggling weed were thick and strong, so that he could rest at times in his climb and lean heavily upon them. Knowing that with every minute that passed his weakness was growing, he did not wait longer than to regain his breath, and then, with a twist of his mouth he forced himself as close as he could to the wall, and engulfed in the dust-smelling darkness of the ivy he began, yet again, to climb.

For how long Steerpike clambered upwards in the acrid darkness, for how long he breathed in the rotten, dry, dust-filled air, is of no consequence compared to the endlessness of the nightmare in his brain. That was the reality, and all he knew, as he neared the window, was that he had been among black leaves for as far back as he could recall—that the ivy stem was dry and coarse and hairy to hold, and that the bitter leaves exuded a pungent and insidious smell.

At times he could see glimpses of the hot evening reflected through the leaves, but for the most part he struggled up in darkness, his knees and knuckles bleeding and his arms weary beyond weariness from the forcing back of the fibrous growth and from tearing the tendrils from his face and clothing.

He could not know that he was nearing the window. Distance, even more than time, had ceased to have any meaning for him, but all at once he found that the leaves were thinning and that blotches of light lay pranked about him. He remembered having observed from below how the ivy had appeared to be less profuse and to lie closer to the wall as it neared the window. The hirsute branches were less dependable now and several had snapped at his weight, so that he was forced to keep to one of the main stems that clung dustily to the wall. Only a foot or two in depth, the ivy lay at his back partially shielding him from the sun. A moment later and he was alone in the sunshine. It was difficult for his fingers to find purchase. Fighting to wedge them between the clinging branches and the wall he moved, inch by inch, upwards. It seemed to him that all his life he had been climbing. All his life he had been ill and tortured. All his life he had been terrified, and red shapes rolled. Hammers were beating and the sweat poured into his eyes.

The questionable gods who had lowered for him from the roof above the prison room that branch of creeper when he was in similar peril were with him again, for as he felt upwards his hand struck a protruding layer of stone. It was the base of a rough window-sill. Steerpike sobbed and forced his body upwards and loosing his hands for a moment from the creeper, he flung his hands over the sill. There he hung, his arms outstretched stiffly before him like a wooden figure, his legs dangling. Then, wriggling feebly, he rolled himself at length over the stone slab, overbalanced, and in a whirl of blackness fell with a crash upon the boarded floor of Fuchsia's secret attic.

3

FLAY-SWELTER FIGHT

He came forward again, sweeping the cleaver in great arcs before him and treading gingerly over the slanting timbers, and then seemed about to halt once more in order to repeat the unwebbing process when, with an obvious change of purpose, he moved forward as though no obstacles were in his path. He seemed to have decided that to be continually reconditioning himself and his weapon during the blood-encounter was ill-advised and untimely, not to say an insult to the occasion.

As pirates in the hot brine-shallows wading, make, face to face, their comber-hindered lunges, sun-blind, fly-agonied, and browed with pearls, so here the timbers leaned, moonlight misled and the rank webs impeded. It was necessary to ignore them—to ignore them as they tickled the face and fastened themselves about the mouth and eyes. To realize that although between the sword and the hand, the hand and the elbow, the elbow and the body, the silvery threads hung like tropical festoons, and although the naked steel was as though delivered in its caul, the limbs were free to move, as free as ever before. The speed of the swung cleaver would in no way be retarded. The secret was to *ignore*.

So Swelter moved forward, growing at each soft, deft pace more and more like something from the deeps where the grey twine-weed coils the sidling sea-cow. Suddenly stepping into a shaft of moonlight he flamed in a network of threads. He peered through a shimmering mesh. He was gossamer.

He concentrated his entire sentience on the killing. He banished all irrelevancies from his canalized mind. His great ham of a face was tickling as though aswarm with insects, but there was no room left in his brain to receive the messages which his nerve endings were presumably delivering—his brain was full. It was full of death.

Flay watched his every step. His long back was inclined forwards like the bole of a sloping conifer. His head was lowered as though he was about to use it as a battering ram. His padded knees were slightly bent. The yards of cloth were now redundant, but there was no opportunity for him to unwind them. The cook was within seven feet of him. Between them lay a fallen beam. About two yards to Swelter's left its extremity had settled into the dust, but to the right, the relic of an old iron box supporting it roughly at its centre, it terminated about three feet up in the air, spilthed with fly-choked webs.

It was towards the support of this beam that Swelter made his way, beating the filigreed moonlight to his knees where it sagged and flared. His path could be traced. He had left behind him, from the door to where he stood, the web-walled canyon of a dream. Standing now, immediately behind the broken box, he had narrowed the distance between them to just over the measure of his arm and cleaver. The air between them was a little clearer. They were closer now than they had ever been this raining night. That dreadful, palpable closeness that can only be felt when there is mutual hatred. Their separate and immediate purposes were identical. What else had they in common? Nothing but the Spiders' Hall about them, the webs, the beams, the byplay of the spangling moon and the drumming of the rain in their ears.

At any other time the chef would have made play with his superior wit. He would have taunted the long, half-crouching figure before him. But now, with blood to be spilt, what did it matter whether or not he incensed his foe? His wit would fall in a more concrete way. It would flash—but in steel. And let his final insult be that Flay could no longer tell an insult from a lamb chop—unless with his body in two pieces he were still able to differentiate.

For a moment they stood, moving a little up and down on their toes. With his sword before him Mr. Flay began to move along his side of the fallen beam, to the left, in order presumably to come to closer grips. As Swelter moved his little eyes to the right following every movement of the other's body, he found that his vision was being impeded by so heavy an interfusion of ancient webbing that it would be unwise for him to remain where he was. In a flash he had both taken a sideways pace to his left and switched his eyes in the same direction. Flay at once crept in upon him, his face half shrouded by the thick webs through which he peered. His head was immediately above the lower end of the beam. Swelter's rapid glance to his left had been fruitful. He had seen the lifted end of the beam as his first true friend in a hall of hindrances, and when his eyes returned to his thin foe his fat lips twisted. Whether such a muscular obscenity could be termed a 'smile' he neither knew nor cared. Mr. Flay was crouching exactly where he had hoped that he might lure him. His chin was, characteristically, jutting forwards—as though this habit had been formed for

Mr. Swelter's convenience alone. There was no time to lose. Swelter was three feet from the raised terminal of the long beam when he sprang. For a moment there was so much flesh and blood in the air that a star changed colour under Saturn's shoulder. He did not land on his feet. He had not intended to. To bring the entire weight of his body down upon the beam-head was all that mattered. He brought it down; and as his under-belly struck, the far end of the beam leapt like a living thing, and, striking Mr. Flay beneath his outstretched jaw, lifted him to his full height before he collapsed, a dead weight, to the floor.

4

THE TWINS

'He said he would exalt us,' said Clarice. 'You heard him, didn't you?'

'I'm not deaf,' said Cora.

'He said we weren't being honoured enough and we must remember who we are. We're Lady Clarice and Cora Groan; that's who we are.'

'Cora and Clarice,' her sister corrected her, 'of Gormen-ghast.'

'But no one is awed when they see us. He said he'd make them be.'

'Make them be what, dear?' Cora had begun to unbend now that she found their thoughts had been identical.

'Make them be awed,' said Clarice. 'That's what they ought to be. Oughtn't they, Cora?'

'Yes; but they won't do it.'

'No. That's what it is,' said Clarice, 'although I tried this morning.'

'What, dear?' said Cora.

'I tried this morning, though,' repeated Clarice.

'Tried what?' asked Cora in a rather patronizing voice.

'You know when I said "I'll go for a saunter"?'

'Yes.' Cora sat down and produced a minute but heavily scented handkerchief from her flat bosom. 'What about it?'

'I didn't go to the bathroom at all.' Clarice sat down suddenly and stiffly. 'I took some ink instead—*black* ink.'

'What for?'

'I won't tell you yet, for the time isn't ripe,' said Clarice importantly; and her nostrils quivered like a mustang's. 'I took the black ink, and I poured it into a jug. There was lots of it. Then I said to myself, what you tell me such a lot, and what I tell you as well, which is that Gertrude is no better than us—in fact, she's not as good because she hasn't got a speck of Groan blood in her veins like we have, but only the common sort that's no use. So I took the ink and I knew what I would do. I didn't tell you because you might have told me not to, and I don't know why I'm telling you now because you may think I was wrong to do it; but it's all over now so it doesn't matter what you think, dear, does it?'

'I don't know yet,' said Cora rather peevishly.

'Well, I knew that Gertrude had to be in the Central Hall to receive the seven most hideous beggars of the Outer Dwellings and pour a lot of oil on them at nine o'clock, so I went through the door of the Central Hall at nine o'clock with my jug full of the ink, and I walked up to her at nine o'clock, but it was not what I wanted because she had a black dress on.'

'What do you mean?' said Cora.

'Well, I was going to pour the ink all over her dress.'

'That would be good, *very* good,' said Cora. 'Did you?'

'Yes,' said Clarice, 'but it didn't show because her dress was black and she didn't see me pouring it, anyway, because she was talking to a starling.'

5

BRANCH AND TITUS

Had a branch broken in any one of the thousand trees that surrounded the water, or had a cone fallen from a pine, the excruciating tension would have snapped. Not a branch broke. Not a cone fell.

In the arms of the woman by the shore the strange child she held began to struggle with a strength that she could not understand. It had reached outward from her breast, outward, over the lake; and as it did so the sky began to blossom in azure and Titus, at the edge of the raft, tore at his necklace with such force that he found it loose in his hands. Then he lifted his head and his single cry froze the multitude that watched him on every side, for it was neither a cry of tears nor of joy; nor was it fear, or even pain—it was a cry that for all its shrillness was unlike the voice of child. And as he cried he swung the necklace across the sparkling water; and as it sank a rainbow curved over Gormenghast and a voice answered him.

A tiny voice. In the absolute stillness it filled the universe— a cry like the single note of a bird. It floated over the water from the Dwellers, from where the woman stood apart from her kind; from the throat of the little child of Keda's womb— the bastard babe, and Titus's foster-sister, lambent with ghost-light.

ROMANTICISM IN POETRY

ANTHOLOGIES OF CONTEMPORARY WRITING

Selected and introduced

by

ALEX COMFORT

PATRICK MacDONOGH

MAURICE LINDSAY

GLYN JONES

ENGLISH POETRY

ALEX COMFORT

ROMANTICISM AND ENGLISH POETRY

I is not possible to consider English romantic writing today in isolation. The poems printed here are chosen only to represent a number of strands in a general tendency—its anarchism, its erotic impulse, its diction at the present moment, its attitude to the war and to past history, and the element in it which I believe to be unique, its combination of the Romantic ideology and cosmology with scientific method and rational interpretation of observed fact. The Romantic is a man who believes that the 'absolute' values of ethics and aesthetics were created by man, for man, are coterminous with man, and have no place in any non-human cosmology, but that their validity, even in face of their impermanence, is none the less for that. In this, he seems to me to approach most closely to the genuinely biological viewpoint, and contemporary Romantics have ceased to hate and distrust science as a source of poetic material and philosophy. I feel that this appears in the visual and intellectual method of some of the work here. My selection also exposes the major faults of the Romantic school at present—its imitativeness, its excessive adjectives, and the state of internal tension which exists in much of its poetic structure.

ALEX COMFORT

EIGHTH ELEGY

THERE was a woman in Asia—whether she merited
death, the birds knew, and the mottled weeds:

but so they bound her hands to the dead hands
the dead and the living into the bound grave

and so against her milkless breasts she felt
the idle sinews harden to a cross:

So his green belly pressed the open rose
of her thighs, and his slack jaw came and went at her lips

through days and nights in darkness. Those who listened
could hear the breathing underneath the stone.

Look down today and see your bedfellow.

Sometimes by night utter mortality
is closer than we know, and speaks to us.

Into the final silence which the jocular
years contrive for those whose life is speech . . .

The flames look down and count the candle's length
bound to the pale wax, golden as a soul—

And there were two who lay beside a river
among the acres of the brown seeds tossing

but the trees laughed at them, and gold-eyed birds
thrust their hard beaks through every hanging leaf—

papery heads that the long grass like flames
will pierce, or rivers carry into the lightless sea:

And there were two, watchers beside a fire
crouching in darkness under the bills of wind

who turned and lost each other in the night
and wandered calling, but the hills were empty.

The candle's flesh is white, the flesh of a girl
melting into time, weeping white coins. Below

the stone, those who were listening, for nine days
heard crying. Every day they came again

until grass hid the edges of the grave.
Look down today and see your bedfellow.

ALEX COMFORT

NOTES FOR MY SON

REMEMBER when you hear them beginning to say Freedom
Look carefully—see who it is that they want you to butcher.

Remember, when you say that the old trick would not have
    fooled you for a moment,
that every time it is the trick which seems new.

Remember that you will have to put in irons
your better nature, if it will desert to them.

Remember, remember their faces—watch them carefully:
for every step you take is on somebody's body.

And every cherry you plant for them is a gibbet,
and every furrow you turn for them is a grave.

Remember, the smell of burning will not sicken you
if they persuade you that it will thaw the world.

Beware, the blood of a child does not smell so bitter
if you have shed it with a high moral purpose.

So that because a woodcutter disobeyed
they will not burn her today nor any day;

So that for lack of a joiner's obedience
the crucifixion will not now take place;

So that when they come to sell you their bloody corruption
You will gather the spit of your chest
And plant it in their faces.

AINSLIE ELLIS

SUPREME ANARCHY

Winter of great snows
O snow why lie so deep
Marching is impossible
Our troops and the enemy freeze still
Before they were marching
War is ended
The cat understands the man
The man has become the cat
For the first time
The masses are lonely
They watch
Through panes of glass
Shot with bloodvessels
For music there is the sound of falling stones
Birth is more terrible than death
For no one dies
The souls wander in the streets
And among the chimneys
Jewish souls hang lanterns
Because the poets have gone eastwards
Eastwards over the desert of the long night
The dung of their horses
Alone
Lies on the white roofs

JOHN HEATH-STUBBS

THE DANCING FLOOR OF BRITOMARTIS

THESE are the king's pleasures—
The just king Minos; stone upon stone,
He stares from his hard cold throne, while the half-grown boys
Beat with their feet in the labyrinth dance
On the tessellate floor, where pictured the pigeon
Flies, and the heron intent on his tarn.
The lights burn low, and a soft flute winds
Through the thickening darkness, and curls
To the limbs of the dancers, where smoke-swirl
Shadows their cinctured loins . . .

Tomorrow there will be another kind of dancing—
In the blare and the glare of the sun and the sand,
The trumpets, the copper-toned drum—
The great bulls led forth, beribboned, their dewlaps flapping,
The opposers advancing with calculated tread—
Young men, subtle and cruel as panthers, dancing
With shadow steps, and the short sharp spear
Poised like a wand; then the sweep of grand horns—
Pain, blood, bowels hanging, brute's masculine lust
so much beef, or the adolescent's neck
Awry, like a poultrier's bird . . .

The just king stares from his canopied throne,
From his sun-stool; can these be his pleasures?

*   *   *   *

O wise king of many towers,
Throned among whorled passages, intricate
As the chambered ear, as the gates of the eye, as the cobweb
Of living nerves—remember Britomartis!

THE DANCING FLOOR OF BRITOMARTIS

Remember the fierce pursuit and the virginal limbs,
The quiver-hung huntress, the piercing-eyed arrogant
Girl with the boar-spear; Oh think of the cliff
The desperate fall, and bleeding and torn those limbs
In the fisherman's net; Oh for pity, remember!

OS MARRON

FROM THE NORTH-COUNTRY—I

I WILL never return; I have never come away
from the man-made pyramidal hills.
The Northern rain runs down a groove worn on my heart,
the white of sweat down a miner's dirt,
for the low sky that covers the land like a sea.

I was afraid, in my childhood,
of old Nanny Greenteeth, hag of the canals,
green slime of the backwaters.
Her breath was the mist of nightmares
and the slap of her black lips on stone
drowned for me the singing flowers of dreams,
the silver bells of infancy.

She was the mouth of the canal;
but the sea of mist has a shoal of mouths
for every fathom, and each sharp lip has gnawed
the Northern moon, the dripping, dropping moon
that rots the bells in towers to rust
and turns the mildewed wheel, fades the poisoned flowers
in black mill pools, and spills into flashes
silver as fish in the darkness.

On country pavements in the rain
the rising moon trickles gold into the gutter;
but when in towns the tyrant whistle
unlooses the pale people, hollowed for coal or cotton,
from the closing walls, the manacle machines,
the yellow lamplight slithers on wet flags
like the severed arms and legs
of monsters under the sea, under the clogs.

FROM THE NORTH-COUNTRY—I

And in the late evening between the dripping lamp-posts
lovers move like bubbles in the fog
quietly as goldfish in a bowl
a pair of planetoids in another universe.

The musty wet skirts of the night
have trailed across the shining slate,
an old woman passing, past desire, worn away
on the lips of the mist, she dabbles fingers,
dribbles light on entries, culs de sac and suicides;
and in the crumbling walls, mumbles over a flower
mother to foetus, seed of all love.

On the moor lie the dreaming lovers
in respite from the sea, the stone-wall lanes,
the closing walls of mills and mines
covered now in memories of rhododendrons,
a singing wind to use their ears as shells,
cornflowers and bluebells to blow in their eyes,
across their whispered loves; and the sly moon
will smile on summer, ever the deceiver,
marble, unapparelled, from the South.

Flowers lie dark in iron parks
and fill the altars of black chapels,
Under the shawl the old mouths every morning move,
the prayers of the old like pearls
are lifted up from the deep of lost desire
in the smoky sun of old sacrifices;
and the children of sunlight sparkle like hope
like apples on the low black hills;
  I will be unafraid
when Northern rain again runs down my heart,
I will never return. I have never come away.

OS MARRON

FROM THE NORTH-COUNTRY—II

Word without music, white as a cross,
I have seen a single seagull, far from the sea
on days when the land leans under the wind,
under the sea of cloud, scream at the sky of grass;
and I have never gone an hour without a stone.

In my youth, in summer, I thought the moors mild,
soft, upthrust, especially under stars,
comparable to a bosom, beneficent as cedars,
but touching now the last strands of that running season,
her wild warm hair, the flowing wind,
I heard behind the lid of winter close,
came to know the inner spine, the Pennine,
and saw the cold wind breaking on its bones
fluttering torn scarves down the sheltered vales
among the pleasant people of the hollowed stone
the shining children in the sombre yards of schools.

These are the friendly vales, though even in such havens
have I seen men take up a stone
and thrust it in their breast for a heart,
swung out from pity, unsoftened by the sea,
a solid world unscoured by the clean North wind
where never a flung gull is graceful
nor the running children like fields of flowers
along the windless shore, the barren sands.

And as the sea will break the stones, so his bones
will toss beneath the land, like the lost bird
under the tumbling clouds, under the sod;
and once will tell of danger to a miner,

the shifting seas of rock, as I was warned of weather
above there on the moorland by a gull;
and the pick will pluck his heart of stone
from the cage of bone that crumbles into dust,
and the sound will be a harp, a star trembling,
and coal will swirl like jewels, like a night sky
down there in the dripping darkness.

Have I breathed ever? here the strong air after the pit
kneads the heart, sharpens eyes to stars,
and picks the lanes clean on the little hills,
closes the flowers in the higher places
turning fragrance in upon itself
that forced out through the breathing moor
is half as sweet again, as when in towns
the warm airs from the bakers cellar
intoxicate the children, hungry as birds
in streets stripped bare by the bitter wind.

Above the land the sky breaks on the pikes,
on the shore the stones are splintered by the sea.
The sun fingers the broken spines, the Pennines,
and the sea presses in from both sides,
the earth from below, under the amazing birds;
and underneath black sunlight seeps through rock
the wind will never wander over, though men may sing
from the hidden heart, soft as the moor in summer
with mouths full of pearls;
    from this mad-eyed darkness
flower and foetus, seeds of all love spring
and gusts of song from chapels in the vale.

OS MARRON

FROM THE NORTH-COUNTRY—III

In summer all lands are the South
and I have known a tropic night of jewels
hang over these counties heavy as fruit,
and by day rhododendrons burst into plumage
among the dark green leaves, along the stony lanes.

In the town the factory, hollow-eyed
flings a black cape down, a Spanish shadow
over streets that burn slow like slag,
bubbling with pitch; only the closed pubs are cool
and the old men marvel at the wine beneath the flags
and spit desire between their clogs
chewing the long hours, the withered figs;
always behind the walls the muttering machines
and whirling belts that scream of tropic birds
deep in a jungle, above the sweating people.
Only at four o'clock breaks a river of blossom,
the singing flowers, children from schools.

Prisoners are not only set in stone,
the wind once blew the imprints of our chains on grass
in the open parks, and over the humpback moor
we heard our fetters ironed by the hard birds
that cried despair through desert afternoons
when lists in public reading-rooms
had sung plain-song over hope in the morning;
it was then the sun sustained us, scorched us dry
of all but dreams, only these remained
hanging bright, heavy with love, the rhododendrons,
fists of flame through the screens of long days
when only eyes were blind to stars.

Once in summer in the kiss of grass
I saw myself above them on the rim of a sphere,
the stars underground, the night sky of coal
where the pick can take a universe in one
and loose the fossil wind, the black planets
in a spittle of nebulae, the Milky Way;
and wheels follow shuttered eyes down tunnels,
the running darkness echoes back a song
along the rails to where the old men bend
under the weight of black light
under the load of earth in the deep pit.

Who love are never bound, never bend,
and those who dream, dream in freedom.
The stone of grey days will not close on us
but always the sun, a bell over the wood
manœuvres into cover every lover
and we are in a hollow breast, a cave of leaves,
blue light in glory from gentleness
a flock of bluebells, white as milk at the stalk
when torn from the earth, the eyes of doves
and innumerable children;
      when again the rain runs down
the white ash of winter on the heart settling
a song of leaves will tremble in the hidden stars
and the light in the shaft a torrent of wings.

NICHOLAS MOORE

CHARLEY DIDN'T HAVE A NEW MASTER

O IN the walking mud of battle, the rattler
Walks like a strange artiste over the graves
Of the uncomfortable and the unseemly brave.

Charley hadn't any money nor any voodoo,
No charm to keep him from the worst of the battle,
He just innocently did what me and you do.

O I'm gonna wash my hands of you, you'd razz
Would you, I'm just another victim, he would sing,
Bowled over by the hot spirit of jazz.

But Charley the saint, Charley the aunt, Charley the martyr,
I salute you and bless you for everything;
Because through all this red and blue murder

You kept the heart you had. In the disaster,
Charley, the unicorn, never had a new master.

NICHOLAS MOORE

THE HAIR'S BREADTH

TELL me, hair of her head, where I should lie
Who wish to praise her in my poetry?
Tell me, hair of her thigh, what should I do
Who wish to make my image of her true?

Dog by the lamp-post, God above the clouds,
Am I to follow either with my words?
Is she a bitch to be by flesh accosted,
Or holy image and by blood attested?

Tell me, hair of her whole anatomy,
With what attentions I may make her happy?
Tell me, hair of her heart, what I can be
To tender her in all world's misery?
The blood of love may flow from me to her,
But how can I describe it by a hair?

PRAYER TO NOBODY, WHO IS SOMETHING

(*For Priscilla*)

Dear Sir and Father, I have been praying . . .
The gooseberry bush is far from the schoolroom's yard,
And they who hand in hand go in the maytime
Have to leave early, and this February ice

Is chilling to the hands and feet, and my heart is tired.
That I took an ill girl into the ditch
Is not to be accounted sin.
I was careful from the first, when I began,

And where I went to among her swaddling clothes.
O, my Lord, she lay in the ditch like an April rose,
And my tongue dropped like an adder into the bush.
It was February and the year was young, the sun

.   .   .   .   .

Was scarcely hot enough to taste, and her eyes
Pulled me down among the dry sticks and the frozen snow,
Lifted up her belly like a bottle to my gaze,
That there below I should see a bush and die.

My Lord, Dear Sir and Father, there go I . . .
And now I look into the bushes of the future,
See a red woman step like a God in the road,
And a mad man lashing thistles with his cane.

This is my festival of prayer. The pain
Is in my legs, and my Achilles heel is stung,
Hung like a cross upon a February ditch,
The snow among, and the sharp flicker of sleet,

PRAYER TO NOBODY, WHO IS SOMETHING

So that I rise in the image of another one,
A splendid and terrible, killed and willing, man.
Do you not see his footsteps in the teazle, Sir,
His remains hanging on the wooden stile like a latch?

I have taken a candle to light him to bed.
There in the sheets of it with my doe I
In the electric shadow lie of the pillow, and
The table with six legs, my switch in your hand,

Am the gooseberry boy, and your husband,
Dear Sir and Father, and Madam-will-you-walk.
I married you on an August morning, alarming
The sound of the sirens, and charming your talk.

I am praying. This is February. And the war lives,
With a man bloody lying on a reckless globe,
The flying hero in a halo of flashes,
A slow people beginning to feel the pinch.

So now, darling, I bless you with each inch,
Who are my wife in the bed and tart in the ditch,
My everything-said-and-done and good-for-nothing girl,
Garbo and witch, whom a dark park bench

Brought me in the easy days, when summer was light,
Dear Sir and Father, History whom I believe,
Fate, Nature, accountable to all men,
Lead us, Earthly Angel, lead us from this dark night

Into a lighter bed and a happier Jerusalem;
For you, above all things, are universal,
A God to those who believe in God,
A party to those who believe in a party,

A Christ to those who believe in a homo,
But not nothing, except to those who have died.
So I pray to you, bless my wife who is you,
And hope the future and you will be forever true.

PAUL POTTS

SELECTIONS FROM A BALLAD FOR BRITONS

THERE was a moment in the world
In seventeen hundred and thirty seven
When the water stood still on the Thames
And men upon the clyde-bank heard
The pulse beats of history hammering out the news
Tom Paine is being born.
Because a man like Paine was born immune
From the festering itch of the branding iron
Of those who make their profits out of men
The working class is now the word made flesh
And Christ hung up on Calvary
Is man on Main street Stalingrad.
The urge for living this man had
First stole the attention of the world
From courtesans and princes
The King is dead
Long live the king
His Majesty King Man.

       *   *   *   *

They called us the mass, the great unwashed
But ours was the dirt of their profits
They found us hard to look upon
Their sins were tattooed on our faces.
We who made the wheels go round
Became the comic section of a clubman's mind
They could only smell our sweat
They could never understand.
'Hands wanted'
Hearts get in the way

But there is a story told in Birmingham
Of how God himself came down
To open wide
The hospitals of heaven
When the girls who worked in the great new mill
Died that night
The owners had an extra contract to fulfil.

       *   *   *   *

For no building, not the Pantheon
No poem, not the Iliad
No painting of the Renaissance
No music even if it is by Bach
Is more important than a man,
The man who scrubbed the deck
That Nelson died on.
The man who grew the wheat
For Alfred's cakes
The man who cleaned Queen Bess's shoes
So leave us alone
And we'll come home
Bringing our dreams behind us.

PAUL POTTS

NO

O BODY of the woman that I love
I held you for a moment in my hands
With both the hunger of a sparrow
For a January crumb
And with the reverence of a Conrad Noel
For the altar bread.
Whirling out beyond the tiles and prison bars
My dear became the capital of the stars.
Down through the years that lead away from there
My life is like some vagrant tent
Waiting for your heart when it is tired.

PAUL POTTS

A POET'S TESTAMENT

GREAT Villon,
Bless this spit
As upwards from the gutter it ascends
Attacking the face of those
Who caused a man to clutch at any kindness
With all the desperation a Jew might use
To hurl his child beyond the frontiers of the Reich

HERBERT READ

TO A CONSCRIPT OF 1940

Qui n'a pas une fois désespéré de l'honneur, ne sera
jamais un héros.—Georges Bernanos

A SOLDIER passed me in the freshly-fallen snow,
  His footsteps muffled, his face unearthly grey;
And my heart gave a sudden leap
  As I gazed on a ghost of five-and-twenty years ago.

I shouted Halt! and my voice had the old accustomed ring
  And he obeyed it as it was obeyed
In the shrouded days when I too was one
  Of an army of young men marching

Into the unknown. He turned towards me and I said:
  'I am one of those who went before you
Five-and-twenty years ago; one of the many who never
    returned,
  Of the many who returned and yet were dead.

'We went where you are going, into the rain and the mud;
  We fought as you will fight
With death and darkness and despair;
  We gave what you will give—our brains and our blood.

'We think we gave in vain. The world was not renewed.
  There was hope in the homestead and anger in the streets
But the old world was restored and we returned
  To the dreary field and workshop, and the immemorial feud

'Of rich and poor. Our victory was our defeat.
  Power was retained where power had been misused
And youth was left to sweep away
  The ashes that the fires had strewn beneath our feet.

'But one thing we learned: there is no glory in the deed
   Until the soldier wears a badge of tarnished braid;
There are heroes who have heard the rally and have seen
   The glitter of a garland round their head.

'Theirs is the hollow victory. They are deceived.
   But you, my brother and my ghost, if you can go
Knowing that there is no reward, no certain use
   In all your sacrifice, their honour is reprieved.

'To fight without hope is to fight with grace,
   The self reconstructed, the false heart repaired.'
Then I turned with a smile, and he answered my salute
   As he stood against the fretted hedge, which was like white
     lace.

STEPHEN SPENDER

THE CONSCRIPT

On the turf's edge, which flashes like a knife,
A conscript stands, above his native city.
He drinks the sun's last rays before that night,
Whose tunnelled throat will swallow up the life
He's known—to thrust him on vastness tomorrow.
The sunset strews the streets below with light.
Deep in the embers of self-pity
His small heart burns within a bowl of sorrow.

The iron wheels of morning seem so real,
The future, crude with knives, is so defined,
That this last hour seems only what he feels
A poignant memory straining through his mind.
The setting sun melts into a gold past
With the pathos of freedom left behind,
Its halo scanned through blackened bars of contrast.

The hill grows pale, the flourishing colours fail,
Then freezing agate seals the city walls.
That schoolyard, where his childhood crowed, is torn
Out of his eyes. The gentle veil
Of night, indifferent to him, falls.

Then his eyes look beyond his fears,
Beyond the stars, to where a scene appears
Of villagers marching to earlier wars.
The skeleton which strides last, strikes a drum.
The conscript's bones ache through his flesh, as, pale,
'Father!' he cries, 'Father! Behold, I come!'

PETER URE

THE WINTER PALACE

To the hollow-held light a cloud advancing
Towards the winter palace with the little skaters,
The windows shutting and the darkness opening
On the rococo its wings of fighters.

Now all the vases stream with lamentation
And the trees their soaking heads thresh
And with a roar the ice is melting,
But empty the pond and the bright scarves.

I see a ship driven and come to land
And down from its carved deck a captain descend.
Seamed with wrinkles his distant eye,
But as he looks and walks, a prince.

Before the blind palace with a continuous voice
The water-drops on the terraces dance:
In his eyes the long front with ornaments and windows
Is reflected in one image as he remembers.

PETER URE

IN THE CITY

THE water is in the town, and the glaucous
Eyes look through the lovers' flesh at the mending air,
The bodies of sailors drag among these shops,
Over their mouths the weeds, and the pull under their feet.

The young men look dumb; the girls like poppies
Flare and flourish walking in tiers of three,
But the waves press their skirts on their thighs
And the naked mermen grin from the corners of streets.

A bell winging could heave the water to shudders,
But a sterile ocean possesses and rocks the city:
The sailor feels the strength drain from his body,
And the girls have all lain with mermen secretly.

IRISH POETRY

PATRICK MacDONOGH

ROMANTICISM AND IRISH POETRY

SOMEBODY (was it Byron?) once wrote a long letter because
he had not time to write a short one, and it would be
easier to select a couple of hundred than a dozen poems
to illustrate the romantic tendency in recent Irish poetry. For
romanticism, as widely interpreted in the editor's brief, is
characteristic of most of the verse written in Ireland in this
century. Irish poets are, as a rule, anti-mechanical, free in
their work from literary or political ideologies, concerned
directly with earth and the human spirit. Partly because this
is not, even yet, an industrial country, but also by character
and tradition, they show small inclination to deal directly
with contemporary social or political questions, or even to
present the phenomena of contemporary city life. That is not
to say that they neglect these things, any more than such a
poet as Austin Clarke neglects the pressing moral and spiritual
problems of contemporary Ireland. It is a question of method.
The Irish poet brings his raw materials to the alembic of
personality and distils from it something rich and strange. It
is the essence he seeks. Whether speaking as himself or, as
very frequently, out of an adopted personality, he speaks as
an individualist out of an introspective mood in which he has
dwelt with passionate intensity upon the speaker's thought
until poetry emerges, personal, intense, passionate. As Padraic
Fallon has somewhere said, poets in Ireland tend to make of
every common street a Via Dolorosa, and the combination of a
brooding inward attentiveness with delight in visible nature

has produced a poetry at once spiritual and sensuous. Poems so begotten, however intricate their form, however laboriously wrought over, retain the unity imposed by a central creative impulse and remain records of real emotional experiences. Thus Irish poetry has avoided the eccentric movement, as it has eschewed the flashy effects and fashionable tricks, of some English schools. In the best poetry of the Celtic Twilight, for all its delicacy, myth and legend and dream stood firmly upon 'fundamental brainwork' and human experience, and there was more actuality, more humanity, in it than in all the 'realistic' or 'intellectual' poetry recently written. And among later Irish poets, those who turn (as F. R. Higgins did, as Austin Clarke, Robert Farren, Padraic Fallon, and others are doing) to the 'cold, hard, yet passionate realism' of medieval Gaelic poetry, and its richly sensuous music, are writing a verse which, for better or worse, is unlike anything before done in English in its mixture of sharp visual imagery, lusty masculine humanity, ironic humour, and never-resting, often contorted, spiritual searching. These poets are, by modern standards, highly productive and their peculiar qualities are displayed only in poems too long to be included here.

Obviously any proper representation of recent Irish romantic poetry is impossible in the space allowed. Firstly, this selection contains nothing which first appeared before 1937. Secondly, no women were admitted, and so there is nothing by Rhoda Coghill or Temple Lane, to mention only two. Thirdly, only living poets were included and so there is nothing by F. R. Higgins or Joseph Campbell. And fourthly, all Irish writers were ruled out who are not now living in Ireland and publishing work here—Colum, Stephens, Gogarty, Frank O'Connor, Day Lewis, and how many more! Thus it comes that of the men who first gave the country a national literature in English, the only representative is Seumas O'Sullivan. There could be none better, and certain of 'the sort now growing up' might do well to learn from his poem '1939' that strength and grace are not, after all, incompatible.

There has been some public lamentation lately over the

poor quality and quantity of the recent poetic output in Ireland. Certainly the wind that was blowing sparks to flame in the earlier years of the century blows no more, but the output is not so poor either in quantity or quality as the mourners proclaim. In Northern Ireland there has been a remarkable outburst of activity in the arts, and W. R. Rodgers, Roy McFadden, Maurice James Craig, John Irvine, John Hewitt, and Robert Greacen are only a few of the poets contributing to it. There is in some quarters, north and south, a tendency to create a literary as well as a political and economic border; but northern writers show no more readiness than southern to surrender their individualities to 'schools' of verse, although some, by the content of their work, might be grouped as 'Ulster Regionalists'. Others, perhaps inevitably, are closer to English than to Irish mood and idiom, but among southern writers too there are some like Valentin Iremonger (recently awarded the 'Æ' Memorial Prize) who are as English as the English themselves. This, however unfortunate for the preservation of an Irish national literature in English, does not in itself make their poetry better or worse, or necessarily kill the romantic tendency in it. Some poets in both parts of the country alternate between near-English and definitely Irish writing, and some, whose verse-forms and vocabulary have nothing peculiar to this country, are yet positively and unmistakably in the Irish mode. Lyle Donaghy, for instance, a poet whose work has still to be properly assessed, writes now in a stylized, monumental English, yet persistently reveals an un-English quality, and Patrick Kavanagh, with no recourse to Gaelic models, is always recognizably Irish, not only in his poems on peasant themes, such as 'The Great Hunger', but in all his work.

Even after the application of the 'rules of exclusion' already mentioned it remained obviously impossible to give any kind of representative selection in the space allowed. All that has been done is to get together a few poems by outstanding or easily accessible poets of different types, with a preponderance of young poets. The selection cannot even plead the usual, and only, justification for the anthologist, but I am not the less grateful to those who have generously allowed me to use their work. It is to be hoped that the poems which follow may be accepted as random pointers to a varied and not inconsiderable region of modern literature in the English tongue.

AUSTIN CLARKE

THE LUCKY COIN

COLLECT the silver on a Sunday,
Weigh the pennies of the poor,
His soul can make a man afraid
And yet thought will endure.
But who can find by any chance
A coin of noble shape
That never came from Salamanca
Or danced on chapel plate?

Though time is slipping through all fingers
And body cannot stay,
That lucky coin, I heard men tell it,
Had glittered once in Galway
And crowds were elbowing the spirit
While every counter shone,
Forgetting grief until the ages
Had changed it for a song.

Turning in cartwheels on the fairground,
The sun was hastier
That strolling girls might have for dowry
Two hands about the waist;
The men still voted for O'Connell
After the booths were closed,
And only a few in Limerick
Remembered their own souls.

On Nephin many a knot was tied,
The sweet in tongue made free there,
Lovers forgot on the mountain-side
The stern law of the clergy

That kiss, pinch, squeeze, hug, smack denied,
Forgot the evil, harm
And scandal that come closer, lying
In one another's arms.

Not one of us will ever find
That coin of noble shape
For it was lost before our rising
Or stolen—as some say.
But when our dread of the unseen
Has rifled hole and corner,
How shall we praise the men that freed us
From everything but thought?

J. LYLE DONAGHY

PASTORALE

In seas of loveliness we move awhile
and greatest loveliness is human nature given to love,—
the flowers had candid blossoms and their petals
    blue and white finished-finishless were boundless bourne of
      light
my loved one chained me with a living smile,
the wind has hostings of delight among the white clouds' race
    and in the spiced grove of interior tree—
my loved one leaped into my arms with wild sweet ecstasy—

In seas of loveliness we move awhile
and gentler-true because we know the years are brief—
and love is passionate which yields upon the lips imprinted
    the soul's shape in a kiss,
and there is quiet like the white of flowers
    which is most full of life—
and there is beauty in the blossoming of hours
that to their fresh perfection wax quietly
and leave, each one, a perfume in their place.

PADRAIC FALLON

from

RAFTERY'S DISPUTE WITH THE WHISKEY

(after the Irish of Antony Raftery)

If you shortened many a road and put a halo
On every thought that was growing in my head,
Have I not been to you as the brown nut to the hazel,
Your fruit, O my comrade?
And in many a lonely bed have I not praised you
With sleepy words no virgin ever heard?
And after all this, O the spite of it, here in Kilchreest
You topple a tallow candle and burn my beard.

Troy in its tall sticks never burned with a blaze
As bright as Raftery's hairs when that evil spark
Leaped on his skull and from that holy rooftree
Pitchforked his spluttering thatch;
Shame on you! not even Mercury who rose
Out of the cradle to fall on evil ways,
Stealing cattle, would hobble my wits and roast them
Hide and hair like that in the fire of my face.

O I was the sight then and the great commotion;
Wells running dry and poor people peeling their legs
With barrels and pails, and the fish flying down to the ocean;
And look at me now! a mere plaster of white of eggs!
Look at me! A bonfire to folly! but no man
Was ever a saint till he was a sinner first;
And I'll break with you now though it cost me the mannerly
    company
Of the gay talkers who follow a thirst.

RAFTERY'S DISPUTE WITH THE WHISKEY

So I dismiss you. Here take your mouth from my mouth!
I have weighed you, O creature of air, and the weighman cries,
'Here's nothing will balance a holding of land in the south,
Beef on the hoof there and the grass climbing up to the skies;
What's whiskey to hanging bacon?
To a glittering hearth and blue delphware?
Will it put a Sunday coat on any man,
I ask you, or leave him to walk bare?'

Ah, sweet whisperer, my dear wanton, I
Have followed you shawled in your warmth, since I left the
    breast,
Been toady for you and pet bully,
And a woeful heartscald to the parish priest;
And look! If I took the mint by storm and spent it,
Heaping on you in one wild night the dazzle of a king's whore,
And returned next morning with no money for a curer,
Your publican would throw me out the door.

ROBERT FARREN
(ROIBEÁRD O FARACHÁIN)

THE ECSTASY OF COLMCILLE

Colmcille walking
with the Spirit in His lofty places,
apples in his mouth from His orchard
and the flavour of the nuts from His boughs.

Colm out at Hinba, on the swivel of the shifting waters,
beached for three days such a ground-sea pouring of grace
that the flesh felt the feasting of the soul and was not wanting,
and the world had its end at his walls, with its darks and days.
In a house out of time, lit with milk-bright air, Colm, single
and singing spirit-songs like no song string-twanged or
    intoned,
and the light weaving out on the day-shine, like gleamy silver
on dun-coloured shale, or like crystal on mist-dim stones.

Colm piercing in through the images and skins of clay-things
clearing them like glass one haws and polishes with rags;
and solving riddles of the Scriptures; and arcana of ages
spreading to the wide-eyed soul like a high-flung flag.

Colmcille walking
with the Spirit in His lofty places,
daylight in the mind, shine of the day-without-end.

Colm wishing Bahan beside him in his house out of time
to quill down the daylight for men stick-tapping in the dark,
Bahan being limberer and firmer of finger; but the isle
of Egea was his jail for those days, and the jail of his bark.

Colmcille walking
with the Spirit in His lofty places,
his life like a draining inkhorn that lets the quills.

ROBERT GREACEN

THIS ALIEN WORLD

O, I was tense and loving then
When the whole wild grief of autumn swept
And put again her likeness on the rack of memories.
I was taut with fear that summer evening,
Numb as a plate of glass, dead as a cigarette stub,
As fingering the last letter, I stepped into a vacant future,
Knowing no other future than the sunlight on her hair.
Then, for a long dull moment, time ran cold
While rain swished on the indifferent city,
And the ghosts of war sidled through empty streets.
So now, fearing as then for each new future,
I hear the traffic lurch, the windows shiver,
The hurt dogs whine, the brakes pull short. . . .
And now, as then, the fast world tense with reeling
Spins to a stop and leaves me undefended
Against the septic agony of wondering how-and-when. . . .
Sitting and flicking the parchments idly,
I hear the whole wild grief of autumn weeping,
Weeping for lost summers beyond the lost horizons,
Weeping with the torture of this alien world.

JOHN HEWITT

THE GLENS

GROINED by deep glens and walled along the west
by the bare hilltops and the tufted moors,
this rim of arable that ends in foam
has but to drop a leaf or snap a branch
and my hand twitches with the leaping verse
as hazel twig will wrench the straining wrists
for untapped jet that thrusts beneath the sod.

Not these my people, of a vainer faith
and a more violent lineage. My dead
lie in the steepled hillock of Kilmore
in a fat country rich with bloom and fruit.
My days, the busy days I owe the world,
are bound to paved unerring roads and rooms
heavy with talk of politics and art.
I cannot spare more than a common phrase
of crops and weather when I pace these lanes
and pause at hedge gap spying on their skill
so many fences stretch between our minds.

I fear their creed as we have always feared
the lifted hand between the mind and truth.
I know their savage history of wrong
and would at moments lend an eager voice,
if voice avail, to set that tally straight.

And yet no other corner in this land
offers in shape and colour all I need
for sight to torch the mind with living light.

VALENTIN IREMONGER

POEM

ALL evening, while the summer trees were crying
Their sudden realization of the spring's sad death,
Somewhere a clock was ticking and we heard it here
In the sun-porch, where we sat so long, buying
Thoughts for a penny from each other. Near
Enough it was and loud to make us talk beneath our breath.

And a time for quiet talking it was, to be sure, although
The rain would have drowned the sound of our combined
    voices.
The spring of our youth that night suddenly dried,
And summer filled the veins of our life like slow
Water into creeks edging. Like the trees, you cried.
Autumn and winter, you said, had so many disguises

And how could we be always on the watch to plot
A true perspective for each minute's value? I couldn't reply,
So many of my days toppled into the past, unnoticed.
Silence like sorrow multiplied around you, a lot
Of whose days counted so much. My heart revolted
That Time for you should be such a treacherous ally

And though, midnight inclining bells over the city
With a shower of sound like tambourines of Spain
Gay in the teeth of the night air, I thought
Of a man who said the truth was in the pity,
Somehow, under the night's punched curtain, I was lost.
I only knew the pity and the pain.

JOHN IRVINE

THE SOLDIERS

GONE with the stricken armies
They ride to distant country,
Where never one will know them
On mountain or on plain.

Rich fields they left behind them,
Their flocks to stray untended,
And followed in the twilight
A bugle on the hill.

PATRICK KAVANAGH

from

THE GREAT HUNGER

THE pull is on the traces, it is March
And a cold black wind is blowing from Dundalk.
The twisting sod rolls over on her back—
The virgin screams before the irresistible sock.
No worry on Maguire's mind this day
Except that he forgot to bring his matches . . .
'Hop back there Polly, hoy back, woa, wae'.
From every second hill a neighbour watches
With all the sharpened interest of rivalry.
Yet sometimes when the sun comes through a gap
These men see God the Father in a tree:
The Holy Spirit is the rising sap,
And Christ will be the green leaves that will come
At Easter from the sealed and guarded tomb.

Primroses and the unearthly start of ferns
Among the blackthorn shadows in the ditch,
A dead sparrow and an old waistcoat. Maguire learns
As the horses turn slowly round the which is which
Of love and fear and things brought half to mind.
He stands between the plough-handles and he sees
At the end of a long furrow his name signed
Among the poets' prostitutes'. With all miseries
He is one. Here with the unfortunate
Who for half moments of paradise
Pay out good days and wait and wait
For sunlight-woven cloaks. O to be wise
As respectability that knows the price of all things
And marks God's truth in pounds and pence and farthings.

DONAGH MacDONAGH

MIGRANT

WHAT mettlesome wind will carry me out of Ireland
Blown like a feathered speck fast into foreign countries
Where eyes can see a new landscape and ears
Weary of jingled halfpence of sound may hear
A richer coinage rung on the graded marble?
On top of the gale I'd voyage far in a morning
Making towards the ripe, sunlighted evening and a landscape
Splashed and dazzled with colour, and people not withered
With keeping body and soul together through the bitter
    season.
But what wind is there that will call to the eager bird
That watches puzzled the migrants without plot or compass
Steer headlong for the brightness and the trees spreadeagled
To catch the sun as it bounds unbroken through the plain of
    the sky?
What wind is there but the thin and bitter east
Driving the creature into the ragged thatch
To watch the long rain, firm as the bars of a cage?

PATRICK MacDONOGH

THE WIDOW OF DRYNAM

I STAND in my door and look over the low fields of Drynam.
No man but the one man has known me, no child but the one
Grew big at my breast and what are my sorrows beside
That pride and that glory? I come from devotions on Sunday
And leave them to pity or spite, and though I who had music
　　have none
But crying of seagulls at morning and calling of curlew at
　　night
I wake and remember my beauty and think of my son
Who would stare the loud fools into silence
And rip the dull parish asunder.

Small wonder indeed he was wild with breeding and beauty
And why would my proud lad not straighten his back from the
　　plough?
My son was not got and I bound in a cold bed of duty
Nor led to the side of the road by some clay-clabbered lout!
No, but rapt by a passionate poet away from the dancers
To curtains and silver and firelight.
O wisely and gently he drew down the pale shell of satin
And all the bright evening's adornment and clad me
Again in the garment of glory, the joy of his eyes.

I stand in my door and look over the low fields of Drynam
When skies move westward, the way he will come from the
　　war;
Maybe on a morning of March when a thin sun is shining
And starlings have blackened the thorn,
He will come, my bright limb of glory, my mettlesome wild
　　one,

With coin in his pocket and tales on the tip of his tongue;
And the proud ones that slight me will bring back forgotten
  politeness
To see me abroad on the roads with my son,
The two of us laughing together or stepping in silence.

ROY McFADDEN

ELEGY

Now autumn pauses in these Antrim lanes,
Pulling the red leaves sadly, one by one,
His footprints visible in morning fields
When the hills are bowed in prayer, and the mists wheel
Seaward, scattering from the mists of sun.

The beautiful is the most sorrowful,
Lacking eternity. The tree that falls,
Broken and splendid on a wind-ploughed hill,
Cradled in grass, falls in the murmuring heart,
Leaving the black wound there, and all its leaves
Spatter the mind with childish pitying hands.

Now as the last leaves fall her eyes are closed.
She, who was beautiful, is in the trees,
And her beauty drops with the leaves, and her sad smile
Lurks in the clouds that stare from hill to hill,
Over the damp fields and white, patched farms,
The grey hands folded now, those eager hands
That builded me, and bled for others too.

But somewhere, on some pale twist of a road,
She will be walking, towards an unknown town,
Past strange fields and unfamiliar hills,
Nervous maybe, and maybe quite alone
When evening thickens and the night draws on;
Carrying memories of this other town,
Its knotted roads and wayward countryside,
And the suns flowering in the passive trees
That outlive all the storms that humble them.

SEUMAS O'SULLIVAN

1939

Where are the powers that fought for us
In days ill-starred and dark as these?
The sudden rapture, and the kiss
In the mid-battle's dearest stress?
And laughter, powerful to control
The dread accidia of the soul?

How can *we* pray to these for aid
(Like those who stood at Salamis,
In sacrificial joy arrayed,
And eager for the last dread bliss)
Who bear upon each sad doomed head
The mark of beasts to slaughter led?

Look then within; there only lies
Our only hope, and there the prize
Of our sad calling; only there
The secret message, and the fair
Illumining, that yet may start
The lure of the unconquered heart.

BRUCE WILLIAMSON

POEM

WHO would have thought
That so much night was hidden in one garden?
It must have poured from every hollow root
And crooked stem,
From all the ravenous and gaping flowers
So early in defeat.
An hour ago, dear, and you would have seen
Your shadow pave your way
From here, out to that ring of trees,
And a fenland of other shadows
Sinking the ground before you,
Spreading and deepening
Until it reached your knees.
And you would have thought and been right,
'This is death by drowning'.

Once in the sunlight, too, you were aware
Of peril for us both.
You held me closer and you claimed
Love could be nothing loth
To sunder us before we kissed again.
The moted cataracts of light
Shone out through hedge and briar,
And then you said, dear, and were right,
'This is death by fire'.

Doomed constancy! they cried, the wise ones,
And chuckled in their graves.
The snouted monsters reared and beckoned
Within our tired heads.
Fidelity! Ah, Constancy! The bells ring over us.
The azure tides of love recede,
Destructive, purposeless.

MAURICE LINDSAY

ROMANTICISM AND SCOTTISH POETRY

T HESE overworked terms 'Classical' and 'Romantic' have been turned and twisted to so many strained uses that any writer who still proposes to employ them must first offer his definitions. By 'romantic', as applied to poetry, I mean poetry in which the qualities of the emotions are not restricted by those of the intellect in the texture of the work; by 'classical', poetry wherein more or less rigid intellectual conventions prohibit the free exercise of the imagination.

Classical art can only flourish upon prosperous native economic conditions such as have rarely been allowed to prevail in Scotland.[1] Scottish poetry knew no Augustan age. The northern Augustans were mainly concerned with the diverting business of vitriolic criticism which they practised with such avidity in their various Edinburgh reviews. James Thomson, the one outstanding poet amongst them, moved southwards and became a disciple of Twickenham. In any case, his discovery of Nature as a suitable subject for poetry (and to illustrate solid Scottish homilies!) sounded the tocsin for the Augustans, and heralded the ideas of the English Lake Poets. The artificial prosperity of the nineteenth century was merely a temporary English backwash; and although, during the Victorian era, Scotland excelled in the building of locomotives and ships, her poetry reached its absolute nadir.

Scottish poetry, then, is fundamentally romantic in character. An examination of the work of the last twenty-five years, the poetry of the Scottish Renaissance, shows that it is deeply rooted in things traditional, and that the problems which have

beset Scottish poets for five hundred years present themselves
anew to her poets today.

The romanticism in Scottish poetry is partly a strange union
of opposites—a sensitive and painstaking faithfulness to
nature, on the one hand; a delightful 'confusion of the senses'
which leads either into dreamland or hearty, fantastic merry-
making, on the other. To some extent, this manifestation of
the 'Caledonian antisyzygy' is a result of the blending of two
racial strains—the Gaelic-speaking Highlander, and the Low-
lander with his 'Inglis' contacts.

Faithfulness to nature is an essential part of all romantic
creeds. And the trout in Gavin Douglas's stream, those

> *silver scalit fishes on the greit*
> *Ourthwart clear streamis sprinkland for the heat,*
> *With finnis shinand brown as synopar*
> *And chisel tailis steerand here and thar,*[2]

or James Thomson's[3] frightened hare who

> *sits*
> *Concealed with folded ears, unsleeping eyes*
> *By Nature raised to take the horizon in,*
> *And head couched close betwixt her hairy feet*
> *In act to spring away*

are no less carefully drawn than Adam Drinan's[4]

> *Long blue shadow of salmon lying,*
> *shot shell of leaping silver,*
> *using the lull and the flies*
> *to practise for the rough river.*

'The forest solitude,' says Matthew Arnold,[5] 'the bubbling
spring, the wild flowers are everywhere in romance.' He goes
so far as to claim that English poetry owes its turn for 'catching
and rendering the charm of nature in a wonderfully near and
vivid way' to a Celtic source. In Scottish poetry there can be no
doubt whatever. The continual presence of nature is part of
the Celtic tradition; but the precision of the drawing is a
Lowland quality.

The other marked romantic characteristic, the 'confusion of the senses' which leads directly to things not of this world, or to worldly situations seen from a humorous or novel angle, has been an essential ingredient of Scottish poetry since Dunbar,[6] dreaming,

> ... *saw approach, agayn the orient sky,*
> *A sail, als quhite as blossum upon spray,*
> *Wyth merse of gold, brycht as the stern of day,*

and his anonymous contemporary[7] described the giant Gog Magog who

> *wald upon his tais up stand*
> *And tak the starnis doun with his hand,*
> *And set them in a gold garland*
> *Aboif his wyvis hair.*

Allan Ramsay, Robert Fergusson, and Burns himself were all masters of the humorous *genre* piece, touched with fantastic satire.

> *Braid Claith lends fouk an unco heese,*
> *Maks mony kail-worms butterflies,*
> *Gives mony a doctor his degrees*
> *For little skaith:*
> *In short, you may be what you please*
> *Wi' gude Braid Claith,*[8]

said Fergusson; and in recent times there has been no lack of this kind of Scottishness in the work of Violet Jacob, Hugh MacDiarmid, Alexander Gray, Douglas Young and many others.

To say that comparative economic poverty and the existence of two never quite reconciled traditions are the main reasons for the wide-sweeping romanticism which pervades all Scottish poetry would be to over-simplify. Scotland's violent history is full of romance, and Wallace, Bruce, John Knox, and Mary of Scots are more vividly alive in the mind of the Scot than any historical character is in the English mind. This is largely due to Sir Walter Scott, who, although no accurate historian, presented the atmosphere surrounding his country's historical characters so convincingly that the *Waverley Novels* form an Everyman's introduction to the Scottish past. Probably his influence is felt less by those who write poetry than by those who read it, for most poets will pursue their history to its sources. But as a result of the influence of the *Waverley Novels,* the Scottish mind is 'conditioned' to expect an historical sense in its poets.

Although the Scot is keenly aware of his past, he is not always so in the right way. It is strange that, in a country where there are so many scarred stones and cairn-marked battlefields to remind of former greatness and glory, this sense of history should exist quite independently of political nationalist feelings. The majority of people in Scotland who read *Old Mortality* and thrill to the deeds of the persecuted Covenanters, or who sing the innumerable laments for the departure of Prince Charlie, have little or no concern for the affairs of contemporary Scotland. The Scots sense of history all too often turns out to be but maudlin sentimentality for old things irrespective of their merit. It was the triumph of such an attitude, allied to the imitative, unintelligent adulation of the fresh and spontaneous romanticism of Burns's songs, which proved the utter undoing of Scottish poetry in the nineteenth century. This sense of history, therefore, is capable of producing the worst pages of 'Whistlebinkie' as well as such magnificent poems as 'The Brus', 'Schir William Wallace', or, in more modern times, William Bell Scott's 'Holyrood', and many of Edwin Muir's finest poems.

Political nationalism has revived during the last twenty-five years, alongside the Scottish literary Renaissance from which it has gained strength, and in turn, inspired. It has been a potent force in Scottish poetry from 'The Brus' onwards. In the years following the union with England, of course, when most Scotsmen were endeavouring to become anglified, it became much diluted, although it revived indirectly with Ramsay and Burns. In their wakes, 1715 and 1745 brought great waves of nationalism amongst Gaelic poets. The chief danger nowadays is that the political element too often comes before the artistic, and the result is broadsheet doggerel of the 'workers rise and break your bonds' variety. Hugh MacDiarmid, Douglas Young, and Sydney Smith have, with varying degrees of success, risen above this difficulty, and produced some poetry of a high order inspired by nationalism. The very fact that it utters the aspirations of a minority—for only a small part of Scotland's population is as yet awakened to the imperative need for self-government again, if the country is not to become only a neglected English province—gives the political poetry of the Renaissance a romantic flavouring. The best songs of Smith which urge the nationalist claims are also the suffused expression of the human desire for 'abstract' freedom, and as such have a universality.

> *O the winter's been lang, my luve, my luve,*
> *Frae this northern lan the sun's bin awa,*
> *We've aa got weary o' waitan, my luv,*
> *For the days of thaw.*
>
> .   .   .   .
>
> *O the glory's uprising, my luve, my luve,*
> *Ye can hear Scotlan's hert pulsin fierce wi the Spring,*
> *They'll no silence this music again, my luve,*
> *Howe'er they ding!*
>
> *For we've waited owre lang, my luve, my luve,*
> *As they wh'd thwart an' constrain us'll see,*
> *Aye, we've each the richt o' a man, my luve,*
> *Tae gang free!*[9]

Since the new Apocalyptic movement broke surface a few years ago, there has been a continuous eddy of excited Scottish chatter over its alleged English origin. Despite the fact that nearly all the original writers of the group were Scottish, Welsh, or Cornish, and despite the obvious kinship with the Celtic 'confusion of the senses' traditions, its imagery and its allusions, Scottish[10] critics have denied its Celtic relationship, and accused it of being an English-fathered bastard of French

Surrealism. Now that the movement, as such, has disintegrated and the writers stand on their own, it is easy to see that J. F. Hendry, one of the erstwhile leaders, possesses many non-apocalyptic Scottish virtues. But the essential qualities of his work, his careful selection of brilliant imagery, his mastery of vocables, his mysticism, and the burning passion which under-lies all expressions of his thought are Celtic to the core. Perhaps the essential difference between romanticism in Welsh and Scottish poetry[11] is that whereas the mystical, prophetic 'Druid' element is stronger in the Welsh, it is replaced by the more earthy delight in nature of the Scottish. If this is so, the wayward mysticism of much of the Apocalyptic writing, whilst being Celtic in influence, is Welsh–Celtic rather than Scottish.

All the poets of any significance in Scotland today are Romantics. Despite Hugh MacDiarmid's assertions to the contrary,[12] for most Scottish poets, the resolving of the 'Caledonian antisyzygy' is still the first and greatest problem. It is inherently a romantic problem, involving the fusion of influences which are far from complementary. The outward sign of this inward struggle is the language problem. Most of the so-called Scottish Chaucerians whose Scots we now turn back to were so misguided as to call their language 'Inglis'. The aureate, enamelled atmosphere of much of their work was a romantic convention, and their language was not that of the ordinary people. The poets of the second Scots revival, which began with Allan Ramsay and reached its culminating peak in Burns, latterly used a much denser Scots; but most of their words were still fairly common currency. During the bleak years of the nineteenth century, the influence of Burns-the-sentimental-moralist dominated poetic activity. With the gradual anglification of the country—a process which spread outwards from the towns until the advent of the B.B.C. and the cinema—Scots became thinner. When Hugh MacDiarmid 'founded' the Scottish Renaissance and determined to write in Scots, he had to compound his own Scots from the various sur-viving dialects. His achievement is nothing short of miracu-lous. In him and in him alone the 'Caledonian antisyzygy' comes near to resolution. But his achievement is a personal one. The greatness of his poetry has stirred the poetic forces latent in the Scottish genius, and the result has been the present Renaissance which, although still in its infancy, bids fair to rival the two great periods of the past. Yet this revival is spread over three languages. His formulae have not proved the open sesame to those who have tried to put them to similar use. It is the stature of the poet's mind and not his choice of language which has exerted such a singular influence.

Although a newer, English-writing tradition has sprung up and a large proportion of Scottish people speak English, the English-writing Scot is never a completely satisfied man, however much he may pretend to be. His English is, of course, English 'with a difference', but it can never achieve the rich, broad vowel-music of Scots, nor the overtones of national association which cling to the native tongue.

The Gaelic-writing poet is in a still worse predicament. Of the 140,000 remaining Gaelic speakers, only a minute percentage read poetry. And whilst a Gaelic resurgence is still a practical possibility, it would depend largely upon official encouragement and sympathy, not likely to be forthcoming from a predominantly English government.

The problem is one to which I am sure there is no general answer. MacDiarmid's declaration that 'we Scottish poets must needs travel back . . . into Scots and Gaelic. Anglo-Saxon is not for us' comes nearest to the truth. We must refresh ourselves at the Scots and Gaelic springs, then face the problem looking forwards, not backwards. The English wedge can never be driven out. That is sufficient justification for writing in English. But unless something happens, the Gaelic poet will only be read in translation in the future. Unless something happens, the Scots-writing poets grouped around MacDiarmid may come to be regarded years hence as the perpetrators of a romantic convention as far removed from everyday life as the convention of the Scottish Chaucerians. That 'something' is the re-establishment of a Scottish government within a measurable number of years. Most of the young poets are keenly aware of this situation, and many of them are consequently active in politics as well as literature.

Without self-government to check the destruction by neglect of all that is best and most characteristic in Scottish life and letters, there can be no truly national literature in the future Scotland. Meanwhile, it does not matter much what language poets employ, as long as they are convinced that they are giving of their best for Scotland. If this third Scottish revival is not to be the last, Scotland must regain control of her own affairs: for a nation that is disenfranchised permanently and integrated in a more powerful neighbour state cannot long exist as a separate cultural entity.

Such is the position in Scotland today. And in such an atmosphere, romanticism flourishes in its widest aspects.

POSTSCRIPT

Since writing the above article, I have come back to Scotland after six years' military exile. Many of my views have changed —I am now convinced that it is quite impossible for a Scottish poet to express both himself and Scotland fully other than in Gaelic or Scots. An inner compulsion has moved me away from English myself, and in recent months all that I have written has been in Scots. Nor do I any longer believe in the 'poverty-stricken' myth spread about by those who seek to undermine the resurgence of Scottish National feeling. Scotland has always been and could be today self-supporting. But if her rapidly decaying economy is not soon to collapse altogether, she will have to get back control of her own affairs. In the last few years, realization of this has become more widespread, but Nationalist feeling has not yet found a wholly effective way of overcoming the wealthy and well-organized forces of predominantly English Unionism and Trade Unionism which keep it down by making each other out to be the dangerous bogy if Scotland were ever to have her own Government.

The anthology which follows, therefore, is more Anglo-

Scottish and less Scottish than it ought to be to be fully representative of recent and growing trends. New poets who use
Scots have arisen, the most considerable being Alexander Scott,
and George Campbell Hay, the Gaelic poet, has also taken to
writing in Scots on occasion.

[1] From the point of view of Scottish literature, 'modern' Scotland dates from
about 1350. The earliest extant piece of Scottish verse laments the death of King
Alexander the Third, an event which took place in 1290.

[2] Gavin Douglas, Prologue to Book xii, *Aeneid*.

[3] James Thomson, 'Autumn', *The Seasons*. Allan Ramsay, although he relapsed
into the Augustan manner when occasion suited, cannot be considered a true
Augustan.

[4] Adam Drinan, 'The Ghosts of the Strath'.

[5] Matthew Arnold, *The Study of Celtic Literature*.

[6] William Dunbar, 'The Golden Targe'.

[7] Anonymous, 'Ane Litill Interlud' (sometimes attributed to Dunbar).

[8] Robert Fergusson, 'Braid Claith'.

[9] Sydney Smith, 'Skail Wind'.

[10] A contention offered by several of Scotland's leading literary figures, but
one which I do not share. To my mind, it is utterly absurd, and merely convinces
me that the northern mind is incapable of understanding Surrealist *abandon*; not
that much of value is lost through such an inability.

[11] I use the word in a rhetorical rather than a literal sense. For some years I
have held the private view that there is a strong Celtic feeling in Blake's prophetic
poems, despite their Semitic settings and allusions

[12] Introduction to *The Goldern Treasury of Scottish Poetry*.

DOUGLAS YOUNG

HIELANT WOMAN
(frae the Gaelic o Sorley MacLean)

Hae ye seen her, ye unco Jew,
ye that they caa Ae Son o God?
Thon trauchlit woman i the far vine-yaird,
saw ye the likes o her on your road?

A creefu o corn upo her spaul,
swyte on her brou, saut swyte on her cheek,
a yirthen pat on the tap o her heid,
her laigh-bouit heid, dwaiblie and sick.

Ye haena seen her, ye son o the vricht,
wi 'King o Glory' fowk roose ye weel,
on the staney westland machars thonder
swytan under her wechtit creel.

This spring o the year is by and gane
and twenty springs afore it spent,
sin she's hikeit creels o cauld wrack
for her bairns' meat and the laird's rent.

Twenty hairsts hae dwineit awa,
she's tint her simmer's gowden grace,
while the sair trauchle o the black wark
pleud its rigg on her clear face.

Her puir saul is eternallie tint,
as threeps aye your kindly Kirk;
and endless wark has brocht her corp
to the graff's peace, lown and derk.

Her time gaed by like black sleek
throu an auld thaikit hous-rig seepan;
she bruikit aye sair black wark,
and gray the nicht is her lang sleepan.

HUGH MacDIARMID

TWO MEMORIES

RELIGION? Huh! Whenever I hear the word
It brings two memories back to my mind.
Choose between them and tell me which
You think the better model for mankind.

Fresh blood scares sleeping cows worse than anything else on
    earth.
An unseen rider leans far out from his horse with a freshly-
    skinned
Weaner's hide in his hands, turning and twisting the hairy
    slimy thing
And throwing the blood abroad on the wind.
A brilliant flash of lightning crashes into the heavens.
It reveals the earth in a strange yellow-green light,
Alluring yet repelling, that distorts the immediate foreground
And makes the gray and remote distance odious to the sight.

And a great mass of wraithlike objects on the bed ground
Seems to upheave, to move, to rise, to fold and undulate
In a wavelike mobility that extends to an alarming distance.
The cows have ceased to rest; they are getting to their feet.

Another flash of lightning shows a fantastic and fearsome
    vision.
Like the branches of some enormous grotesque sprawling
    plant
A forest of long horns waves, and countless faces
Turn into the air, unspeakably weird and gaunt.

The stroke of white fire is reflected back
To the heavens from thousands of bulging eyeballs,
And into the heart of any man who sees
This diabolical mirroring of the lightning numbing fear falls.

TWO MEMORIES

Is such a stampede your idea for the human race?
Haven't we milled in it long enough? My second memory
Is of a flight of wild swans. Glorious white birds in the blue
    October heights
Over the surly unrest of the ocean! Their passing is more than
    music to me
And from their wings descends, and in my heart triumphantly
    peals,
The old loveliness of earth that both affirms and heals.

J. F. HENDRY

THE SHIP

Here is a ship you made
Out of my breast and sides
As I lay dead in the yards
Under the hammers.

Here is the hull you built
Out of a heart of salt,
Sky-rent, the prey of birds
Strung on the longshore.

Here is her rigging bound
Nerve, sinew, ice and wind
Blowing through the night
The starred dew of beads.

Here her ribs of silver
Once steerless in a culvert
Climb the laddered centuries
To hide a cloud in a frame.

ADAM DRINAN

SUCCESSFUL SCOT

Gold pins and pearls of Columba,
 how gross they grow by your drive,
studding an English summer
 with the back-end of your life,
 beknighted and pompous Scot!

By adding figure to figure
 you have developed never,
you have just grown bigger and bigger
 like this wee wort from the heather;
 and size is all you have got.

Your mind set toward London,
 your belly pushing to success,
from the very day that you won
 the Bursary of the West,
 have flagged and faltered not.

Not much has your face altered!
 The man has the mouth of the child.
The position you planted and watered
 expands from the lad's desires
 as if bound in a pot.

And would you return (for the fishing)
 to your island of humbler hours,
there in your tailored wishes
 you would trample your youth in this flower
 that you have forgotten:

or spending a stay-at-home summer,
 you will never know what they suffer,
these bloated flowers of Columba;
 you will own the youth of others,
 and never know what.

SYDNEY GOODSIR SMITH

CAN I FORGET?

CAN I forget the sickle mune
Owre Largo throu the driven clouds
The sea lik bilan milk at oor fit?
Can I forget the snaw aroun
An the tent-flap lik a gun boom
Whan the wund tuik it?

Can I forget the wolves' houl
Famished rinnan throu the toun
O haar an frost an gaslicht?
Can I forget the staucheran news
As Christ received the Spainish doom
An nocht we did but drink o nichts?

Can I forget ma black wound?
Kirkcudbright may ye be dung doun
An damned Dundrennan too;
Can I forget, och never, a luve
Crottle in my twa hauns tae stour,
The rose o ma hert wormed wi rue?

Can I forget the Solway flows
Gray as daith, or the worm i the rose?
Whiles, whiles; but it bides its hour.
Och, thornèd nou, hert's fánatic pouer
Strang as the skaith it stranger flouers
—The skaith's a meisure o the luve.

Can I forget whit the saul can prove,
That luve is bricht as the skaith is dure,
The skaith is deep as the luve is hie?
Can I forget I'll neer can lose
Twa tyger een nae mair nor those
Lang houghs lik the silken dunes o the sea?

CAN I FORGET?

Can I forget, ma luve, ma luve,
Havana thrang wi drucken fules
An ye amang them, lauchan quean?
Can I forget, ma luve, ma luve,
Strathyre's muckle bed in a wee room,
White breists lik hills i the mune's lily leam?

Can I forget the gifts o you,
Music thats the wine o luve,
The wund an sea-burds in your hair?
Can I forget, ma pouter-doo,
Voar an winter an hairst are you,
Sun an mune an the warld, ma dear?

MAURICE LINDSAY

THE STORM

A SHRIEKING wind, all day hysterical,
fumbled the house, and every window-pane
shook as the impotent fingers gripped and slipped
on the smooth, clean surface, wet with running rain.

Tight, sticky buds of March wept restlessly
over the soaked, earth-spattered daffodils;
the steady, lashing raindrops hissed and seethed
on the gravel paths and gurgled away in rills.

Through the ringing storm, a single church-bell tolled,
goading the faithful up on the hill to pray
for the sins of the world, and the nagging, personal sins
that only His cruel death could cancel away.

We stood on the shore, where the white Atlantic waves
rattled and sucked the noisy pebble stones,
till even the moist, receptive earth seemed stirred
and the shifting beach was the restless, turning bones

of the simple dead; the farmers and fishers who stay
in their green, forgotten graves; the historic dead,
Melville and Knox, whose black and thunderous words,
like the dragon's teeth, grew wars when they were said;

Mary of Scots, who felt the axe's blade
twice on her neck before it finally severed
her folly from her smooth and Gallic charm;
Montrose, who smelt Death's breath yet never wavered;

and all the violent hosts whose deeds have made
the mental fabric draped behind our blood;
those who have burned as martyrs, or endured
harsh tortures for their stern, exacting God.

THE STORM

I turned to tell her of these heraldic thoughts,
but I could not speak, for suddenly I was aware
of her young, unhindered loveliness as the wind
and the driving rain swept through her streaming hair.

She was poised on the storm like an agile ship's keen prow
when I covered her splendid mouth with the passionate stains
of my eager kisses, and knew in my turbulent heart
such a wild, glad moment as this was shot with the pains

of the past, the ageless, yearned-for ecstatic hover
which will not ever be caught and held to the breast;
so I cried aloud with the hurt of centuries
that beauty never can be wholly possessed.

DOUGLAS YOUNG

ICE-FLUMES OWREGIE THEIR LADES

Gangan my lane amang the caulkstane alps
   That glower abune the Oetztal in Tirol
I wan awa heich up amang the scalps
   O snawy mountains where the wind blew cauld
Owre the reoch scarnoch and sparse jenepere,
   Wi soldanellas smoort aneath the snaw,
And purpie crocus whaur the grund was clear,
   Rinnan tae fleur in their brief simmer thaw,
   And auntran gairs o reid alproses, sweir tae blaw.

And syne I cam up til a braid ice-flume,
   Spelderan doun frae aff the Wildspitz shouther,
A frozen sea; crustit wi rigid spume,
   Owredichtit whiles wi sherp and skinklan pouther
Frae a licht yowden-drift o snaw or hail,
   Clortit by avalanche debris, gaigit deep
Wi oorie reoch crevasses, whaur the pale
   Draps o sun-heated ice ooze doun and dreep
   Intil the friction-bed, whaur drumlie horrors sleep.

They say ice-flumes maun aa owregie their lades,
   And corps o men win out ae day tae licht.[1]
Warsslan remorseless doun reluctant grades
   The canny flumes hain their cauld victims ticht.
But nae for aye. Thretty or fowrty year
   A corse may ligg afore his weirdit tyde
And yet keep tryst. Whiles they reappear
   Gey carnwath-like the wey the glaciers glide,[2]
   Whiles an intact young man confronts a crineit bryde.[3]

158

ICE-FLUMES OWREGIE THEIR LADES

A Lausanne pastor wi's Greek lexicon
    Vanished awa amang the Diablerets,
Syne eftir twenty years the Zanfleuron
    Owregya the baith o them til the licht o day,
Still at the Greekan o't.[4] Twa Tirolese,
    Faan doun a gaig, ate what they had til eat,
Scryveit their fowk at hame, and syne at ease
    Stertit piquet. Baith had the selfsame seat
Saxteen year eftir, but their game was nae complete.[5]

In Norroway in 1792
    Frae fifty year liggan aneath the ice
A herd appeared, and syne beguid tae thaw
    And gaed about as souple, swack and wyce
As when he fell frae sicht i thon crevasse.[6]
    Sae sall it be wi Scotland. She was free,
Through aa the warld weel kent, a sonsy lass,
    Whill whummlet in Historie's flume. But sune we'll see
    Her livan bouk back i the licht. Juist byde a wee.

[1] Professor Forbes o St. Andrews was the first prophet anent glacial deliveries. In 1858 he foretauld the reappearance about 1860 o three spielers tint i the Boissons flume o Mont Blanc in 1820. Frae 1861 till 1865 they appeared in three instalments, as calculate by Forbes, 9,000 feet frae the scene o the mishanter.
[2] In 1914 Sydney King disappearit on Mount Cook, New Zealand, and in 1939 cam out three inches thick.
[3] At Grindelwald a Mr. Webster was engulphit on his hinnymune and eftir 21 year gien back til his widdaw.
[4] In 1917 Pastor Schneider gaed aff amang the Diablerets; in 1938 the Zanfleuron glacier owregya him, and the fowk kent him by his dictionar.
[5] In 1919 Peter Freuchen and anither chiel fell intil a crevasse in Tirol, and in 1935 were fand perfitly intact, ilk ane haudan a partlie playit haund o the cairts.
[6] This and the ither orra information I deriveit frae Mr. Frank Illingworth's article in *Chambers's Journal*, August 1942. Gin it had been mair circumstantial my verses wald hae been mair circumstantial as weel.

RUTHVEN TODD

THE IMPROBABLE SOLUTION

ONCE the names of places were magic
And evocative, a city's dream of spring,
Green shadows on the boulevard, or the tragic
Newspaper cutting, emotionless type declaring
A destruction or a captivity, so many thousand
Dead, or under the shadow of a pitiless hand.

So very much of death, an unknown number
Cowering beneath so great a load of terror,
Have slowed the nimble heart, are stale lumber
In the attic of a mind given too much to error,
And all the names which history relates
Remain, despite our efforts, confined by dates.

So, my dear, I would see a human face
Hold in its gentleness more than the name
Which has wound a spell about each place;
See in a tear the pity and the shame
Of not one, but a million unhappy hearts
From which no shred of agony departs.

Throughout the years the fist of memory clenches,
But in the frustration of one wish or one desire
Lies the unluckiness of many whom love wrenches
This way and that, now cold, now by the fire:
I would see beyond hurt eyes and taunting lip
The hidden cargo of the wandered human ship.

'Love's not Time's fool', though the unlucky heart
Is fool enough to jig to any stupid measure
That desire plays. A look is not a poison dart

But merely anaesthetic. Truly, unhappiness is treasure
Stored in Time's thief-proof vault, giving again
Of melancholy, perhaps, but no cause of pain.

My dear, through our own glass every action
Of another is judged; the distortion of tears
Dried by Time, shows up the enormous fraction
Of error, and as the months melt into years,
The overflowing disaster becomes an incident,
Cleared by memory of all malice and ill intent.

GEORGE BRUCE

THE FISHERMAN

As he comes from one of those small houses
Set within the curve of the low cliff
For a moment he pauses
Foot on step at the low lintel
Before fronting wind and sun.
He carries out from within something of the dark
Concealed by heavy curtain.
Or held within the ship under hatches.

Yet with what assurance
The compact body moves,
Head pressed to wind,
His being at an angle
As to anticipate the lurch of earth.

Who is he to contain night
And still walk stubborn
Holding the ground with light feet
And with a careless gait?
Perhaps a cataract of light floods,
Perhaps the apostolic flame.
Whatever it may be
The road takes him from us.
Now the pier is his, now the tide.

G. S. FRASER

EGYPT

W<small>HO</small> knows the lights at last, who knows the cities
And the unloving hands upon the thighs
Would yet return to his home-town pretties
For the shy finger-tips and sidelong eyes.

Who knows the world, the flesh, the compromises
Would go back to the theory in the book:
Who knows the place the poster advertises
Back to the poster for another look.

But nets the fellah spreads beside the river
Where the green waters criss-cross in the sun
End certain migratory hopes for ever:
In that white light, all shadows are undone.

The desert slays. But safe from Allah's Justice
Where the bread of His Mercy lies,
Where ground for labour, or where scope for lust is,
The crooked and tall and cunning cities rise.

The green Nile irrigates a barren region,
All the coarse palms are ankle-deep in sand:
No love roots deep, though easy loves are legion;
The heart's as hot and hungry as the hand.

In airless evenings, at the café table,
The soldier sips his thick sweet coffee:
The dry grounds, like the moral to my fable,
Are bitter at the bottom of the cup.

EDWIN MUIR

A BIRTHDAY

I NEVER felt so much
Since I have at all
The tingling smell and touch
Of dogrose and sweet briar,
Nettles against the wall,
All sours and sweets that grow
Together or apart
In hedge or marsh or ditch.
I gather to my heart
Beast, insect, flower, earth, water, fire
In absolute desire
As fifty years ago.

Acceptance, gratitude:
The first look and the last
When all between has passed
Restore ingenuous good,
That seeks no personal end
Nor strives to mar or mend.

Before I touched the food
Sweetness ensnared my tongue;
Before I saw the wood
I loved each nook and bend,
The track going right and wrong;
Before I took the road
Direction ravished my soul.
Now that I can discern
It whole or almost whole,
Acceptance and gratitude
Like memories return
And stand where first they stood

GLOSSARY

aa	all	*haar*	sea-mist
abune	above	*hain*	preserve
alprose	Alpine rhododendron	*hairsts*	harvests
als	as	*hauns*	hands
auntran gairs		*heese*	lift up
	occasional patches	*heich*	high
bides	awaits	*heid*	head
bilan	boiling	*houghs*	thighs
bouit	feeble		
breists	breasts	*ice-flumes*	glaciers
bruckit	neglected		
brycht	bright	*jenepere*	junipers
byde	stay		
		lades	loads
carnworth-like		*laigh*	low
	distorted	*lauchen-quean*	
caulkstane	limestone		laughing girl
clortit	dirtied	*liggin*	lying
corp	body	*lown*	calm
corse	animate corpse		
creefu	enough to fill a creel	*maun*	must
crineit	shrunken	*meisure*	measure
crottle	crumble	*muckle*	big
derk	dark	*nicht*	night
drucken	drunken		
drumlie	troubled	*oorie*	chill
dung doun	battered down	*ourthwart*	athwart
dure	severe	*owregya*	gave up
dwablie	infirm		
dwineit	died down	*pat*	pot
		pleud	ploughed
een	eyes	*pouer*	power
eftir	after	*pouter-doo*	pouter pigeon
fit	feet	*quhite*	white
flumes	glaciers		
		reoch	rough
gaigit	fissured	*rigg*	furrow
glower	stare	*roose*	extol
graff	grave		
greit	gravel		

165

saul	soul	*thrang*	crowd
scarnoch	scree	*thwart*	frustrate
shouther	shoulder	*trauchlit*	worn down with
skaith	wound		toiling
skinklan	glittering		
smoort	smothered	*voar*	spring
sonsy	plump, good-natured	*vricht*	carpenter
spaul	limb		
spelderan	sprawling	*warslan*	struggling
staucheran	staggering	*wechtit*	weighed
stour	dust	*weirdit*	fated
swack	abundant	*whaur*	where
sweir	lazy	*whiles*	sometimes
swyte	sweat	*whummlit*	overthrown
syne	since		
synopar	red pigment	*yirthen*	earthen
		yowdendrift	
thaikit	thatched		down-driving storm

WELSH POETRY

GLYN JONES

ROMANTICISM AND WELSH POETRY

ALL modern poetry is romantic. The classic poet, it seems to me, is one who is integrated into the society which produced him, who earns his living by writing poetry just as his neighbours earn it by growing corn or shoeing horses.

In mediaeval Wales the poet was an official in the princely court. He had his seat[1] at the table of his lord, alongside the premier, the physician, and the blacksmith who kept edges on the royal weapons. His function was well defined; he had either, according to his rank, to celebrate the prowess of his lord in battle, or to compose poems for the entertainment of the court and the royal family. Before 1282, we are told,[2] every Welsh prince had his own private poet and his court poet. These men learnt the exacting rules of their trade as did their fellow craftsmen in leather or metals. The metres in which they were expected to compose were intricate, and much practice was necessary to handle them with ease and effect. Possibly an apprenticeship was required, possibly attendance at a bardic technical college, before mastery of the difficult medium was achieved. The bard thus qualified did not express his own emotions in his poems after he had received an official appointment. His job was, as I have said, to construct, using the metres that had been taught him, verses celebrating the martial skill of his employer. Inspiration or no inspiration, he

---

[1] The 'chair' which a modern Welsh poet wins for his ode at an *eisteddfod* is really a relic of this.
[2] W. J. Gruffydd, *Dafydd ap Gwilym* (Gwasg Prifysgol Cymru, 1935).

had to deliver the goods. He was essentially the 'maker', and his poetry I should call classical.

I have spoken of conditions in Wales. In England the situation was not perhaps so well defined. Shakespeare, a classical writer in that he provided, and was paid by a community to provide, poetry for them, yet by his transcendental personal greatness becomes half a romantic poet.

The modern poet is always an amateur. If he is lucky he is a *rentier*. If he is unlucky he is a schoolteacher. Instead of taking his poetry for granted as an essential commodity which society will keep him alive to produce, he feels himself too often, *qua* poet, an outcast and even a rebel. He adopts as the badge of this outlawry strange clothes, strange opinions, and strange behaviour. He will even make a virtue of necessity and *accentuate* the differences between himself and the other craftsmen and workers who continue to make a living by their skill. In a clean-shaven age he will wear a beard; in a hard-hatted age he will go bareheaded. If he is offered a paid job to produce poetry, say a Poet Laureateship, he will stipulate that he will accept it only on condition that he does not have to produce any poetry. Thwarted in being a 'maker', he becomes a 'seer'; rejected as the official bard of the tribe, he becomes its unofficial prophet and augur. Since no individual, or movement, or institution will pay him for odes and laudations, or to express vicarious emotions on their behalf, he is driven back upon expressing his own emotions, and praising, or at least writing about, himself (cf. Wordsworth, Whitman, Lawrence). Since no body of technical knowledge has been officially handed down to him, he will invent his own technique. Since no one will read his poems he will write poems that nobody *can* read. Since he does not need to write occasional poetry, and since there is no time limit set by which he has to produce his work, he will wait upon inspiration. And so on. Such is the modern poet, an amateur, a 'seer', a waiter upon the divine afflatus, an agonized producer of unwanted commodities.

The differences between classical and romantic poetry are to be traced to their origins. Romantic poetry will tend to be subjective, experimental, technically freer, more concerned with inspiration and less with adherence to traditional patterns. It seems to me that the Anglo-Welsh poems I have chosen below are all romantic poems. Of necessity. Only a few modern poems, like Mr. Eliot's 'The Rock', are classical. Classicism has now fled to architects, political cartoonists, and advertisement writers.

Although I have already done so privately, I would like here again, publicly, to thank the poets I approached for the courtesy with which they replied to my request for co-operation, and for the readiness with which they responded to it.

IDRIS DAVIES

ONE FEBRUARY EVENING

Now in these mountain grasses beneath a winter sky
I watch the valleys lighted, I hear the curlew cry,
I hear the sorrowful echoes borne from the Severn Sea,
And the dirge of desolation, the sigh of history.

O mountain grasses ignorant of man and all his pain,
Sing in this freezing twilight, murmur to me again
Of the prehistoric aeons, the landscapes pure and bare,
The centuries of silence, the unpolluted air.

O northern winds, my lovers, roar around me where I stand,
A naked creature lonely in a brown and barren land,
And scatter from my memory the weeds of human lore
And make me as cold, as careless, as a wave on a desolate shore.

GEORGE EWART EVANS

THE PURSUIT

THE sea is too turbulent a lake for swans;
Arched neck and curving prow, they cannot glide
And galleon it; no reed-remembering loveliness
No river-comeliness will tame a harsh, irreverent sea
A swan is no swan, no pageant bird
Who kills his blood to tread the ruffled waters:

Two swans broke out of a still harbour.
They sailed towards the mouth, breasting a false calm,
One leading; escaping, Leda-lovely, from her Jove,
Fleeing the torrid arch of his throat, blind
Into a grey, inhospitable sea and cynic wind.

She after the first warning of the quay-spent wave
Deeper curved her modest throat, her head
Sunk back to her body's weight; her feathers all awry.
Then meeting the sea's rebuff, her bones denied
The quiet ripplings of a myriad sunlit ponds and glassy lakes:
All decorous delights and smooth-processing joys;
Of water fanning in a coned, adulatory wake;
Of neck-glancing pride and stately coronet—
And bounded forward, bending her fluttering strength against
    the flood.

Behind her Jove's image came in his lust,
Gaining upon her maiden yea-and-nay;
Till she climbed abrupt, unswanlike on the water,
And wave-flapping fled across the bay.

He saw her flight; and his blood drawing
Him from the calm, met the ninth wave,
Whose thousand angry throats cried out against his love
And turned him back to quiet harbour.

While she remote across the bay,
With drooping head and exiled majesty,
Tossed—beauty's jetsam—fitfully upon the water.

WYN GRIFFITH

two passages from
THE BARREN TREE

YOUTH is an island bright in the sun
across the sea, but there is no returning:
the convoy moves relentlessly into the west
and over the wake the seagulls crying.
Better a hope lost than a life of lying;
of all man's wisdom, truth is best.

Small consolation, but the broken water
glistens against the green stillness
and the clouds are buoyant in the blue.
Thus the vision, this the craving,
and in the no-man's-sea between,
no flashing light, no harbour promised,
no course foretold but as the wind speaks
to the calling birds.

* * * * *

The island recedes, the familiar beauty fades,
brilliant as June once and maiden-fresh,
captive no more the hundred graces
led in delight along the dappled lanes,
with youth exalted in the morning sun.
All this is gone now, and with its daring,
the certain truth, the known shape of language
bright on the lips of men.
Farewell, then.
Time to turn from the dwindling vision,
the grey ghost of failure, the dusk of youth,

knowing that words are laggard movers
out of their time and place, resistant always
to a new meaning. The old hunger stays
to meet the new craving: all else is gone.
It is time to move.

DAVID JONES

from
IN PARENTHESIS

To groves always men come both to their joys and their undoing. Come lightfoot in heart's ease and school-free; walk on a leafy holiday with kindred and kind; come perplexedly with first loves—to tread the tangle frustrated, striking—bruising the green.

Come on night's fall for ambuscade.
Find harbour with a remnant.
Share with the prescribed their unleavened cake.
Come for sweet princes by malignant interests
deprived.
Wait, wait long for—

with the broken men, nest with badger and the martin-cat till such time as he come again, crying the waste for his chosen.

Or come in gathering nuts and may;
or run want-wit in a shirt for the queen's unreason.
Beat boys-bush for Robin and Bobin.
Come with Merlin in his madness, for the pity of it; for the young men reaped like green barley,
for the folly of it.
Seek a way separate and more strait.

Keep date with the genius of the place—come with a weapon or effectual branch—and here this winter copse might well be special to Diana's Jack, for none might attempt it, but by perilous bough-plucking.

ALUN LEWIS

IN HOSPITAL: POONA

Last night I did not fight for sleep
But lay awake from midnight while the world
Turned its slow features to the moving deep
Of darkness, till I knew that you were furled,

Beloved, in the same dark watch as I.
And sixty degrees of longitude beside
Vanished as though a swan in ecstasy
Had spanned the distance from your sleeping side.

And like to swan or moon the whole of Wales
Glided within the parish of my care:
I saw the green tide leap on Cardigan,
Your red yacht riding like a legend there,

And the great mountains, Dafydd and Llewelyn,
Plynlimmon, Cader Idris and Eryri
Threshing the darkness back from head and fin,
And also the small nameless mining valley

Whose slopes are scratched with streets and sprawling graves
Dark in the lap of firwoods and great boulders
Where you lay waiting, listening to the waves—
My hot hands touched your white despondent shoulders
—And then ten thousand miles of daylight grew

Between us, and I heard the wild daws crake
In India's starving throat; whereat I knew
That Time upon the heart can break
But love survives the venom of the snake.

ROLAND MATHIAS

THE BEARERS

WET in the field,
A dull rook preaching
To congregated hecklers in the trees,
And there, behind the text from Maccabees
Red warfare reaching
Into this ground, in upturned blood revealed.

Yet I am home
With handgrip, knowing
Something there is that turns me to the hills,
Some bowel-moving look about me tills
The body going
To growth. I am turned bonewards in this loam.

And when I go,
A burden and bearing,
O long the labour the dark Beacons make
Cloudwise across the south, and me they take
Covertly faring,
An Eginhard over the unfallen snow.

HUW MENAI

AUTUMN

WITH passion ablaze are the hills and a grey sky lowering;
All ominous even to the owl at his lonely mope;
While dew and the rain into hoar and the flake are flowering,
For the grave of the dead, and the cradle of new-born Hope.

And starlings, with plumes like a star-lit night, are
    chattering—
Strong pirates, in loud dispute o'er the sparrow's find;
And leaves of the trembling birch are earthward fluttering,
To work themselves, far away, on the wheels of the wind.

Even Beauty must go, like all else, through the change that's
    unending;
Must go, as the ghost of herself, for the hill's delight,
To haunt the still pools, and to lead all the star hosts
    descending
To drink of their waters sweet with the fall of the night!

KEIDRYCH RHYS

ALARM, ALARM

I REMEMBER vapour-trails over Gillingham—wavy
And the monument to the builder of the Japanese navy,
And oil burning in black columns down Thameshaven way;
Queer happenings on Gravesend range; Croydon's day.

Detling divebombed—and Hawkinge—we got two;
I saw convoys screaming up the Channel's blue.
Connect dodged shells a lamp's smashed splendour with
A boy's M.M. earned defending Martlesham Heath.

A plotting board with one-five-o hostile;
The Italian raid; patrolling the beaches, Deal,
Oxney, Shakespeare Cliff and the invasion warning.
From pier-extension to Dovercourt, Felixstowe in spring!

Joking and blood in a Nissen hut in South Ronaldshay:
The Flow; trips in a drifter to bird-splashed Hoy:
The *Prince of Wales* through an OSDEF telescope;
The leave-boat; a crofter snuffling his stony-crop hope.

Norwich. All this I remember and more oh much more.
Digging planes King's Bench Walk The 'Temple' burning
But nothing nothing that I can compare
To love like a bell through Yarmouth flying!

DYLAN THOMAS

LIGHT BREAKS WHERE NO SUN SHINES

LIGHT breaks where no sun shines;
Where no sea runs, the waters of the heart
Push in their tides;
And, broken ghosts with glowworms in their heads,
The things of light
File through the flesh where no flesh decks the bones.

A candle in the thighs
Warms youth and seed and burns the seeds of age;
Where no seed stirs,
The fruit of man unwrinkles in the stars,
Bright as a fig;
Where no wax is, the candle shows its hairs.

Dawn breaks behind the eyes;
From poles of skull and toe the windy blood
Slides like a sea;
Nor fenced, nor staked, the gushers of the sky
Spout to the rod
Divining in a smile the oil of tears.

Night in the sockets rounds,
Like some pitch moon, the limit of the globes;
Day lights the bone;
Where no cold is, the skinning gales unpin
The winter's robes;
The film of spring is hanging from the lids.

LIGHT BREAKS WHERE NO SUN SHINES

Light breaks on secret lots,
On tips of thought where thoughts smell in the rain;
When logics die,
The secret of the soil grows through the eye,
And blood jumps in the sun;
Above the waste allotments the dawn halts.

VERNON WATKINS

GRIEFS OF THE SEA

It is fitting to mourn dead sailors,
To crown the sea with some wild wreath of foam
On some steep promontory, some cornercliff of Wales
Though the deaf wave hear nothing.

It is fitting to fling off clothing,
To enter the sea with plunge of seawreaths white
Broken by limbs that love the waters, fear the stars,
Though the blind wave grope under eyes that see, limbs that
    wonder,
Though the blind wave grope forward to the sand
With a greedy, silvered hand.

It is a horrible sound, the low wind's whistle
Across the seaweeds on the beach at night.
From stone to stone through hissing caves it passes
Up the curved cliff and shakes the prickly thistle
And spreads its hatred through the grasses.

In spite of that wicked sound
Of the wind that follows us like a scenting hound,
It is fitting on the curved cliff to remember the drowned,
To imagine them clearly for whom the sea no longer cares,
To deny the language of the thistle, to meet their foot-firm
    tread
Across the dark-sown tares
Who were skilful and erect, magnificent types of godhead,
To resist the dogging wind, to accuse the sea-god;
Yet in that gesture of anger we must admit
We were quarrelling with a phantom unawares.

GRIEFS OF THE SEA

For the sea turns whose every drop is counted
And the sand turns whose every grain a holy hour-glass holds
And the weeds turn beneath the sea, the sifted life slips free,
And the wave turns surrendering from its folds
All things that are not sea, and thrown off is the spirit
By the sea, the riderless horse which they once mounted.

ROMANTICISM IN
THE SHORT STORY

Selected and introduced

by

PETER GOFFIN

PETER GOFFIN

ROMANTICISM AND THE SHORT STORY

IN the natural order of animal life the lion is no more important than the lioness; but in the artificial institution of human society a woman may feel inferior merely because she is female. The doctrine of patriarchism, in one guise or another, has for so long conditioned the social consciousness and shaped the destiny of Western civilization that even the simple physiological distinction of sex, as it is applied to our own kind, carries an implication of social inequality: the tacit assumption that the attributes and properties of the male are socially more valuable than those of the female. In patriarchal forms of society, therefore, all the ruling personages, including the Divine Ruler, are male; and it follows that all distinctions drawn between pairs of things or states of being which can be linked, however remotely, with this basic distinction of male and female, will be similarly prejudiced.

There is, for example, the distinction which the psychologist makes when he suggests that the psychic disposition of every human individual, in accordance with his or her prevailing attitude towards the subjective and objective processes, may be described as being either extroverted or introverted. Although the distinction is not meant to imply that any individual can be exclusively of one type, nor, in its proper context, that extroversion is socially more valuable than introversion, we seldom use these terms without this prejudiced social implication. We associate extroversion with the practical man of action, with leadership, strength, and authority; and introversion with mysticism, the romantic dreamer, and the poet. In other words, the terms have come to stand for the power and the passivity which are supposed to summarize the respective attributes of male and female. And it hardly needs saying which of these 'psychological types' enjoys the respect and admiration of the modern authoritarian state.

It remains, however, that human beings are not simply types of extroversion and introversion; nor are they simply male or female. Every human person is in some degree at once man, woman, and child; and the 'political' attitude we adopt towards one another as men and women and children in society, whether we are conscious of it or not, is bound to affect the individual's inner attitude towards the male, female, and child elements of his or her personal being. Clearly, the proper growth and integration of these elements within the individual will not be encouraged by a social system in which the dominant and privileged sex is male; and in which 'science' tramples triumphantly over the vanquished mysteries of birth, love, and death.

Here and there, however, and from time to time, a warning and prophetic voice is raised against those for whom the word 'science' has become a synonym for sanity. 'A totally unmystical world', says Aldous Huxley, 'would be a world totally blind and insane; and', he adds, 'we are dangerously far advanced into the darkness.'

And yet, as history shows, the magnitude of the folly we have committed in the name of God is only equalled by the magnitude of the folly that we are now committing in the name of science. We have forgotten that the most ancient meaning of God is love; and that the simple meaning of the word 'science' is knowledge. If love is blind without knowledge, how blind indeed is knowledge without love.

The consequence of the application of science without the guiding principle of religion, of knowledge without love, is before us. The world is impoverished, barren, and sick unto death. Only the genius of the heart, a romantic revival, can restore equilibrium to our tottering humanity. Not because the heart is superior to the head, but because it is a biological fact that we cannot live by the head alone. If the world were to become totally scientific or totally mystical, human life would wither away as surely as it would in a world totally male or totally female. Totalitarianism of any sort can lead only to total sterility.

At the level of literary politics we find further evidence of the alarming schizophrenic split in human consciousness; the frustration of the feminine within us; the taboo on tenderness. Here, the 'pair of opposites' are named *Classic* and *Romantic*; and, according to the rules of this game, as T. S. Eliot has pointed out, 'to call any work of art "classical" implies either the highest praise or the most contemptuous abuse, according to the party to which one belongs'. For example, those who would discredit romanticism would agree with Mr. Peter Quennell who says that 'romantic literature appeals to that strain of anarchism which inhabits a dark corner of every human mind and is continually advancing the charms of extinction against the claims of life—the beauty of all that is fragmentary and youthful and half-formed as opposed to the compact achievement of adult genius. The augustan spirit is positive, logical, limited; the romantic mood, masochistic and self-destructive.'

But I would say that it is in this strain of anarchism that our hope lies. For it is the 'feminine' strain within every healthy human being; the genius of the heart that will not suffer conscription. If it has been driven to inhabit a dark corner, it is because it cannot meet violence with violence, but must work its gentle magic in its own way. But it is as untrue to say that it is continually advancing the charms of extinction against the claims of life as it would be to say that children are born not of women but of men; or that the creative spirit itself is masochistic and self-destructive.

Fortunately, however, creative writers seldom work at the level of literary politics. Their politics are what Herbert Read calls 'The Politics of the Unpolitical . . . of those who have always striven, whatever their race or condition, for human values and not for national or sectional interests'. It is for this reason that the writings which I have selected for this anthology do not fit easily into a particular category. If I call them 'romantic', I do so because they are not unmystical, not without a strain of anarchism. Indeed, as we know it, the short story is a young art; and what is youthful cannot be unromantic. But all one need say is that these writings are the expressions of compassionate human beings who know intuitively that one becomes typical by being to the utmost degree one's self.

PAUL VINCENT CARROLL

THE VIRGIN AND THE WOMAN

I

MARTIN used to say in his whimsical way to Mary that it must have been a blunder on the part of the Celestial Foreign Office to have dropped him into a family like the Marrons. Mary was the woman Martin loved. She was also the wife of Martin's brother, Andrew. The explanation they gave each other for their coming together was that they were both human in a tradition of brutality, and that humans will find their way to each other. Martin, with his slim body and sensitive nature, was certainly an incongruity in such a house, for the Marrons, sailormen all, had gone down to the sea for generations, believers in tooth and claw, coarse in body and voice, in mind and soul.

Matthew, the second son, lies at the bottom of the Indian Ocean, together with his ship and a cargo of grain; Owen ran disastrously into one of the terrific squalls that occasionally sweep the English Channel in midwinter; Sidney 'had it out' with four mutineers off the Brazilian coast and accounted in person for three of them before dying of wounds as his ship entered Rio; old John, who had fathered them all, furrowed the seas of the two hemispheres for close on forty years, and lived to hand over his wheel to his eldest, Andrew, who was now lying at Bilbao loading up with iron ore. Some months previously he had by sheer brutal appeal swept the virginal Mary Osborne off her feet, and left her in charge of his father, after three months of uncertain matrimonial weather, for a round voyage that included Shanghai, Beirut, Capetown, Bilbao, and Cardiff.

The Marron homestead was a rambling place with rooms smelling strongly of wood-rot and tar, and laden with innumerable models of old ships, and a bewildering collection of odds-and-ends brought home by the brothers from all over the earth. On the walls hung flamboyant prints of storm-tossed ships, and crude sketches of the heads of grisly mariners, but most conspicuous of all—the disconcerting enlarged photographs of the sailormen sons and their father, stolid, stubborn, and scowling out resentfully.

Built on the edge of the cliff and about half a mile from the spray-swept town of Orme Point, with its mean streets and its straggled sections of crazy houses huddled round a windy pier, the Marron homestead symbolized the mentality of its owners by its pre-eminence, as it looked frowningly down on the roofs of humbler dwellings and out over the racing spray of the sea.

No enlarged photograph of Martin hung on the walls in any of the rooms. Neither was there one of the miserable woman who had borne them all, except one searched deep under a pile of rubbish in a moth-eaten drawer in a back room that looked inland on the rolling plains. Here lay a melancholy reproduction of her, on a yellowing surface, half-faded and forlorn.

From the day Martin's boyish fingers smashed one of the many nautical models in the front room, because he 'hated and hated them', old John Marron suspected his wife, and as the boy grew fonder and fonder of reading, and of rambling inward in search of tall, murmuring pines, instead of downward to the beach in search of a legitimate Marron's birthright, the suspicion grew to certainty and his dislike of her to hate.

Before long she broke under the strain of those ruthless eyes with the steel-like lashes above them that were like the teeth of a comb combing her consciousness for what was never there. She lived long enough to be assured that at least she had reproduced her hounded sensitiveness in Martin, and, having prayed that the bud might flower and add itself to the stray wisps of beauty she had discovered in life, passed quietly out.

Martin missed her terribly at first, for there was in him that sprinkling of the feminine that makes a man pliable and adjustable. To Andrew and his father that theory was a damnable heresy. It was an insult to the Marron tradition of blood and brutality. They, therefore, with the frankness of the stupid, denied his legitimacy, and illustrated their contempt for him by hurling him out of their way in the house. When his dogged studying eventually earned him an opening on the *Courier*, a paper published in the nearby seaport of Orsbycove, their contempt was crowned. A Marron that preferred an office stool to an oilskin! A Marron that was born with a book in his fist instead of a marlinespike. Could that be true and Nature remain impeccable? It finally confirmed old John's belief that his wife had fooled him—once. It seared the thick hide of his pride. Once in a swirl of temper he grabbed Martin by the chest and swung him round in a fury. And the taste remained with him.

II

Grasping for some sort of support when the stay of his mother's influence was withdrawn, Martin fell back on Mary Osborne. Mary, like all virgins, was a romanticist. Her young visualization of life along the windy coast was like the grey picture that appeared every week in the *Courier,* with instructions for the children to colour it. The crayons, used to hide its drabness under the blues and reds and the yellows, were romanticism. Life needed romanticism, believed Mary, as Martin believed a man needed as much of the woman in him as would make his personality colourful and flexible.

Now, in Martin, Mary discovered a romanticism of a type not easily translatable by her. His young vehemence of word and gesture she could understand, but his gentleness never, and his habitual silences, sitting with her under flowering foliage, puzzled her. Her young spirit, being virginal, understood as yet only the strong positive urge. The subtler urge mystified it. When, therefore, Martin at times broke his silences to tell her that trees were often more sensitive than human beings to pain and loss, and that hills were often holier than the flaunted spires of great towns, she secretly thought him silly. Once she laughed and saw him smothering the hurt in his eyes. She came covertly to the conclusion that he was effeminate, and when one day he impulsively put his head on her lap as they sat on a cliff, her surmise was confirmed. The pent-up virginity in her could understand his imprisoning of her hands, or his firm fingers forcing her chin upwards till her lips were vulnerable, but his head pressed pityingly against her bosom was to her negative and as yet meaningless. When occasionally he showed her his name in print above a poem or a sketch she was scarcely impressed. Yet when later she saw a snapshot of Andrew in wildly blown oilskins, holding a ship's wheel in a shower of spray, she was thrilled to the heaving of her breasts.

In Andrew's walk, in his swinging arms, his compelling stride, in the brutality of his chiselled features, in the peremptory vibration of his voice, there was that positive reaching out, that popular romanticism she could easily interpret. From afar he thrilled her, nearer to her she trembled, but the trembling was ecstasy. One day he imprisoned her hands and twisted her arms backwards, so that her young body was impelled towards him. In this there was that glimpse of abandonment she had tasted in a diluted way in the imagination. It thrilled and trembled her young being like a reed shaken in the wind. When afterwards he kissed her forcibly till her body panted, she remained against him after he had freed her —helpless and submissive. Martin, seeing all, could say nothing. He let her go.

Soon Martin was to see her coming out of the church on his brother's arm, and the fisherfolk throwing rice and tiny seashells. It made him dislike the squinting spire even more than previously, and turned his mind more fully inward to the torment of his being. The wedding night was a torture to him. On his bed he begged God to let him sleep so that he could escape his imagination. When sleep did come, his imagination ravaged it unspeakably. In the morning he found himself covertly watching Mary. But she gave him no sign, not even meeting the quick glance of his eyes.

III

During the three months that followed, up to the date of Andrew's departure on his circular voyage, Martin—now terribly alone—kept for some masochistic reason a diary of daily events in the Marron household. Only a few quotations need be set down, and parts even of these deleted, in deference to the niceness of contemporary politeness.

Feb. 8th: Found Mary alone and crying. Wouldn't tell me what the matter was. Women sometimes cry like that when they're with child. Christ, it couldn't be that! . . .

Feb. 11th: She looks worn. I've got to find out if it's that. I'll ask her . . . If it is, I think I'll go away to N.Y. . . .

Feb. 12th: Funked it.

Feb. 14th: Ditto. . . . Andrew drunk. Sang 'Shipmates o' Mine'. Tried to lift me by the hair. Terrified.

Feb. 16th: Funked it again . . . Harvey at the office says he can get me to N.Y. buckshee . . .

Feb. 18th: Mary was cleaning windows today and jumped down off a ledge six feet high . . . Would she do that if she was—that way? Got to ask her, that's all. I'm mad.

Feb. 20th: Asked Mary in a roundabout way . . . Told me not to be silly. Feel like a new man now. But I keep doubting. Is she lying to me?

For the week following, the diary becomes so pitifully intimate that it is not quotable. The nearness of Mary to the boy makes it too terrible a study. But from March 7th onwards, I find it more readable.

Mar. 7th: I love Mary. I adore Mary. I love my brother's wife. God, what have I come to? I should have cleared out . . .

Mar. 11th: Tortured . . . Mary, today, looks womanly and sad . . .

Mar. 16th: Told Harvey I wasn't going to N.Y. Spun him a yarn. All nonsense. I'm not going because I love my brother's wife. I'm lost now . . .

Mar. 19th: Read today in a book by Dean Swift, a terrible Irishman of the 18th century, 'Love is a malady, and woman its cursed witch-doctor ...' Is Mary a witch-doctor? ... or the loveliest of all things? ...

Mar. 24th: The old man flung a plate of soup at me today. Andrew lay back and howled. Mary rubbed my neck with carron oil.

Mar. 27th: Mary asked me today, when alone, how my neck was. Her eyes were beautiful and steady ...

Mar. 28th: Mary terribly unhappy this morning ... Are all women unhappy? ...

Mar. 31st: Told Mary I loved her. She just looked at me with her grave eyes and went on washing cups. I kissed the back of her neck ...

Apr. 3rd: Kissed Mary again. She kissed me back, but very lightly ... How quiet and lovely she is now—lovelier than when she was a virgin ... Mary is a steady lamp shining over a tormented sea ...

Before Andrew went off, he took Mary roughly by the arm and kissed her. He made her kiss him back, his eyes fully upon her the while.

'Are you—expectin' anythin'?' he asked of her at length.

She shook her head, looking up at him, a little afraid, but steadily. Old John, ready to accompany Andrew, joined them from the front room.

'It's damned funny, I call it. What have you to say about it?'

'What can I say, except that there's nothing?' said Mary, her voice very quiet. The old fellow, who suspected Mary, laughed as he drew down his cap angularly. Andrew regarded him meaningly.

There was a pause.

'It's maybe,' said Andrew grimly at length to Mary, 'a matter of you winning the first round, eh? But the knock-out is mine. Sleep on that till I get back home.'

Abruptly he took up his kit and stalked off, the old man following with a grunt. Their oilskins flapped noisily in the fresh breeze as they took the steep road down to the town. Mary watched them from the window—huge hulks in the shape of humanity—till a twist of the road rubbed them, as it seemed, out of existence, as being superfluities. She turned to Martin with steady eyes. He came across to her as if bidden, and touched her deferentially.

At Orme Point the old man did not accompany his son to Orsbycove, where Andrew's boat lay, as he had first intended, but, having bade him an almost wordless and yet wholly eloquent good-bye at the railroad station, turned about to negotiate the stiff climb upwards to his now, to him, desolate home. His feeling for his son was jealously and devouringly emotional, and emphasized by the fact of Andrew's ship having been once his own. He was aggressively convinced that a vital and inspiring part of the mariner remains in the wheel from which a stupid age-limit regulation hounds his physical presence. That Andrew, his eldest son, in fact almost his physical and mental reincarnation, now commanded his vessel, and commanded the wheel in which there remained so much of himself, was a tremendous satisfaction to him. Indeed, the love—or whatever it was—between them was no mere cord tied with the conventional family knot, but sharing, as they did, that circular symbol of nautical achievement, it bound them together closer even than blood and kindred.

Heavy with the thought of Andrew, he silently crossed the threshold of his home, and emerged from the toss and tumult of his preoccupations to find Martin's lips on the lips of Andrew's wife, and his arms about her.

For a moment he paused—his resolve mounting the crazy rungs of his thoughts—his hatred of Martin, his convinced suspicions of his dead wife, his instinctive distrust of Mary, his belief that she had outwitted Andrew's desire for a son—till on the topmost rung it flared into precipitate action.

He had now Martin across a bench, tearing at him as if he would release the disputed blood in him and let it drip back to its mongrel source. But Mary kept frustrating him, her firm hands tearing at his oilskins, her body, panting and cat-like, interposing itself, her voice screaming like a swarm of seagulls in his ears. From the welter of sound and forces Martin escaped like a scared rabbit, flying from the house in which, from his first coherent hour, he had been denied his birthright.

With his friend Harvey, in the town, he made a makeshift home, and in the house perched crazily on the edge of a cliff Mary remained, under the watchdogs of scrutiny in a loathed pair of eyes that sleep seemed but rarely to visit.

IV

The lovers were not irrevocably separated. Old John sometimes had to shuffle into Orsbycove to study the whereabouts of the *Carroway*, Andrew's boat. And, occasionally, he drank himself into unconsciousness. At such times they reached out to each other, and now and again Martin's love for her goaded him up the steep road, usually in the wake of his father's stumbling footsteps. In the silence of the kitchen he always took her hands in his own and looked down at her. She was good to look upon, now that she was womanly and grave. She was like a certain tree that he loved in a valley out of sound of the sea—willowy and strong without showing it. It wasn't that she was merely guileless—Martin believed, like his father, that she had deliberately frustrated Andrew's desire for a son —for guilelessness was a negative quality, but her positivism, the alluring steadiness of her gaze, the strength suggested by the poise of her head, all enthralled him. Incidentally, he knew with the lover's instinct that she would give him sons, and the secret thought exalted his stature and ennobled him.

But although she conferred her love on him and gave him her lips to kiss, she had not as yet consented to go to him, and face a world that was ever ready with its branding irons. In addition to this deterrent there was the physical menace of Andrew, who on his return would be sure to seek, not out of love but out of pride, unqualified revenge.

'He might never come home,' Martin said to her one day.

'Men like him always come home,' she said, quietly.

Martin sighed. 'I wonder how it will all end, Mary,' he asked.

'As it is fated to end,' she answered.

Then their eyes met in the circle of their thought, clung and gravened. He crushed her to him suddenly with passion and she felt and shared his need. The shuffle of footsteps on the road made them delve deep into the long grass. A snort, as of a mind for ever running on indignation, came to them, and then the unmistakable flapping of oilskins. Peering, they saw Martin's father. He was quite drunk, and the tails of his old sou'wester were flapping violently about him like the wings of angry birds. But neither drink nor idiosyncrasy could rob him of that picturesque brutality that appeals to the virgin of either sex.

'The yellow scum!' he snorted to the winds, as he passed.

'I'll get in before him and you can slip up later when he's in bed,' said Mary hurriedly, and with a bound was off through the grass. As she left him Martin noticed that the sea was flinging up jets of dazzling spray, and out of its torment were coming rapiers of wind—the advance guards of an imminent storm. He sought shelter under a rock that frowned down on him with a detachment that was unique.

Mary had time to divest herself of her cloak—and of all else, for that matter, that was caressing to her thought—before the old fellow blundered in upon her, fixing her with the peculiar stare of inebriated eyes. This last was by now not unusual to her, and she had learned to suffer it. Yet tonight, he somehow seemed to her other than human—the embodiment of some hateful force her mind flung away from. The very air seemed to become charged with his presence and to take on splashes of sudden fantastic colouring. The roar of the rising wind added to her unrest. She lit the oil lamp with fingers not quite steady, as if in an effort to bring back the natural atmosphere she could understand.

He sprawled sullenly into a heavy chair by the fireplace, his oilskins weirdly about him like diabolical robes, his cap down over his brow. She decided to take him quietly.

'You're late tonight,' she said. 'Where on earth have you been?'

'Down, woman, where the sea spits on things. I like the way it can spit.'

His tone stung her to defence.

'I suppose that means that *you'd* like to spit on *me*?'

'If I had a mind to, I would. You're no good. You'll never be the mother of a man.'

She cooled suddenly, seeing the uselessness of her anger.

'It's time you were in bed,' she said, quietly.

'Bed . . .' He seemed to echo it. 'The prison of the troublesome, eh?' He laughed maddeningly, as if he could read in her that which was hidden. There was a pause, and then he added, proudly, 'You must keep out of my way and not disturb me. I want to sit and think about my—son.' He said the last word emphatically.

'If you were fair at all,' she said, 'you would remember that you have more sons than one.'

The remark roused him to a fury.

'Is every son born of a man's wife *his* son?' he roared. 'Tell me that, woman!'

She countered rapidly. 'Is every woman tied to a brute bound to drown her own nature, and send on nothing of it?'

'You haven't answered me, woman,' he insisted. 'Come on! Can a mongrel be the son of a giant, and truth still be truth?'

Again she realized her helplessness.

'Are you going to bed?' she repeated, calmly.

'Go you. It might be—safer.' The sudden insinuation disconcerted her.

In the tenseness of the pause that followed she realized that rain was pattering on the roof. As she drew the curtains she glimpsed the gathering clouds and the anger of the sea below. On the way to her, she felt, were conflict and hurricane. She shivered, and again asked him to go to bed. His answer took away her breath.

'No bed tonight. I'm expectin' my—son.'

'What? Martin?' she managed to inquire.

His voice came like a sword thrust. 'My—*son*, I said. Andrew.'

'Are you mad?' she protested. 'Didn't the boat leave Bilbao only last night?'

He nodded, strangely. 'It did. It will be rollin' through the Bay o' Biscay now. Rollin', woman—plungin', staggerin' . . .'

Fear came to her now in earnest.

'And how,' she managed to ask, steadily, 'could he be home tonight, stupid?'

His answer was so calm that it frightened her.

'How do I know how, woman? But he'll be home nevertheless.'

She tried by protestation to reason away her fear. 'You're talking in your sleep, old man.'

'I mustn't sleep. If Andrew were to sleep at that wheel now . . .'

'Well, you're not Andrew. You should be in bed.'

'Maybe I *am* Andrew. Maybe in a way we are one another.' His voice lost its harshness, but not its sinisterness. 'Isn't that wheel of Andrew's *my* wheel?'

'Oh, go to bed,' she entreated. 'What's in that?'

'In it?' he retorted, resentfully. 'There's part o' me, woman, in that wheel. As there's part o' the dead in the things they leave.'

In an agony of impatience she flung up her hands.

'Oh, why am I arguing here with an old fool that the sleep's drowning?' she cried.

The word shot him directly upright in the chair, his eyes on her startled. 'What in hell word is that, woman?'

'I just said the sleep was drowning you,' she answered, a little afraid of his attitude.

He held her for a moment with his eyes in thrall, then, as if overpowered by recurring sleepiness, lay back impotently.

'Sleep and water,' she heard him muttering. 'The two tyrants. The one like a cursed woman, quiet and murderin'— the other like a man, terrible but fair . . .'

The sleep—or was it sleep?—seemed to fall about him like

a veil that made him meaningless and uncanny to Mary. His eyes, although still lidless, became unseeing. It seemed to her that he was sinking down into some horrible shell that hid powers and values not of her knowing. She became conscious of the growth of her uneasiness. Simultaneous with the deepening of the silence inside came the heightening of the wind—fury without, and the one made the other more awful. She felt as if, in a strange way, the blacks of hate and the whites of love were whirling over and over down some hill of conflicts and that at its feet lay racing waters that would resolve all things finally. The swirl of the sea joined now with the gathering furies, and she knew how the trees were leaning over to the stunted walls and sobbing like human beings.

V

As soon as Martin pushed the door inwards, and stood wind-beaten and drenched before her, it all suddenly translated itself to her in one word—conflict. And the conflict was imminent. In what shape it would present itself to her she was vaguely aware. She was, woman-like, piecing together—Martin, the sleeper, the chair, herself, and—Andrew, the last-named though he was myriads of miles from the lists. And still more strangely, she found her intuition insistent upon the inclusion of the dead Marrons as well. She saw them momentarily as Macbeth saw the forms stretched out and out. . . . They touched her consciousness and were made potent in her mind. The battle, she sensed, would be more than physical, more even than mental—a thing shot through with forces she had hitherto not met or felt. Yet she was calm, and Martin saw how quiet and steady her eyes were.

She took his hand silently in her own and led him in, so that he could see the fitful slumber of the old man. Martin's face in the yellow lamplight was weak and small—small enough to be insignificant to one less human than Mary. There were lines upon it that, as a woman, she knew the meaning of. They touched her pity and her protective instinct. She looked at him out of her tranquil eyes, and miraculously she loved him. The thought made her a taut, leashed life-force wrapped incongruously in soft flesh.

'What made you let him sleep there?' Martin asked, in a whisper.

'He wouldn't move for me,' she answered. She caught his sleeve secretively, and her voice was tense. 'He said Andrew was coming home tonight.'

She felt the jerk of his body, and saw his face discolour in the yellow rays, and his gaze turn backwards towards the door. He was suddenly afraid.

'Tonight?' he said, his breath hurting him. 'But that is impossible.'

'I know,' Mary answered. 'But he kept on saying it as if . . .'

'As if what?'

'As if he were sure.' She looked at him fixedly, as if she wanted with all her heart to impart some of her strength to him. 'You must hold on to yourself—hard, Martin. Do you hear?'

'But, Mary, there's no—no danger, is there? How could there be?' His lips were twitching nervously and his face had no colour now. 'Do you know, I—I think that cursed row outside is going for my nerves.'

'If there is danger,' she answered him, steadily, 'we can overcome it together.'

The head of the sleeper lurched a little as if it were borne on a heaving medium. She drew him silently into the shadow cast by a dresser of insect-eaten wood. A branch of a tree crashed down the wind. They heard it hurtling past the window. It was a symbol of brutality, and as such they recognized it unerringly. Martin gave an involuntary sob.

'That's how they would treat *me*,' he muttered. 'That tree was me, and the wind was them.'

The old man's breath increased into weird speech. His eyes, still open, saw nothing of them, but only what was flung to him over wild distance by the potency of some perverted affinity. He seemed uncannily inspired.

'Lift her to it, Andrew,' came his terrible low crying. 'Lift her to it man. It's comin', son, and you're right in the way of it. . . . Don't do that, man. Leave that to the scum aft. Marron blood, eh? It's hell, but keep your eyes forward there, Andrew Marron, as I bred it in you, I, John Marron, senior. Hold her, lift her, lift her to it, man! Lift her, by the red blood in ye, son! . . . Lift! Lift! . . . Phew! . . . A couple of points now . . . Steady! Good! . . . Drenched, eh? . . . What in hell about? . . . Hold that wheel o' mine, Andrew, son . . .'

They listened to him, spellbound, as if witnessing the conflict of ship and water. Martin was visibly trembling.

'He's seeing the ship,' he managed to whisper. A frenzied patter of rain on the roof whisked the rest of his words away on the tumult. Mary was leaning forward, intently listening. 'They were so—close, the two of them,' she heard him sob in her ear. 'Maybe he can see. . . . There's such things, Mary, isn't there?'

'There's nothing we need fear,' she said, calmly, taking his hand firmly to her side. Yet, in spite of her calmness, she was alert in every nerve, and her being seemed in torment. With a start he saw that she too had come to believe. It was not raving, then, or a drunk man's talk, but inspired reaching-out. She was now straining forward as if in a theatre, caught up in the dramatic movement.

'Hi, there!' came the raucous voice again. 'Where's the hangdogs that were workin' the pumps? Scum! Scum! Hold her up to it, Andrew! . . . Hit that yellow cur one in the spine. . . . That's it. . . . He was no good. Scum! Muck! . . . They're taking to the boats, the sons of whores! . . . She's—God! She's —she's goin' . . . Hold her, for God's sake . . . Look it straight in the face! Spit on it, man! That's it! Bravo! . . . It's blood that tells, Andrew Marron. The rest of a man is muck! . . .

So intense and uncanny had the atmosphere become that Martin would have fallen down in fear but for the wiry, capable arm of his companion. The swirl of the waters from without lifted his imagination into frenzy.

'They hate me, they hate me,' he sobbed. 'That poor devil

got his spine smashed because there was a little of the woman in him to make him human. That would have been me, Mary —me, me! Over the side and to hell with me! Oh, God! . . .'

He would have cried aloud hysterically but for her hand on his mouth.

'Hush,' she said, tensely. 'He said it was—going. I—must know . . .' She leaned forward. 'Look, look! He's gasping as if he was struggling in icy water.'

'Does that mean——' Martin began, but she stopped him.

'Listen.'

The raving voice was now strangely pathetic.

'Aye, son, you're nearly home now . . . Marron blood, eh? . . . Sailormen all, they went their way . . . Strange lights, them, Andrew, eh? . . . And the Cap'n's on the pier. Ready, son, salute! . . . Aye, Cap'n, he was a son o' mine—a Marron, if you understand . . .'

The voice ceased on the night. The head fell back as if with finality. A sudden whirl of wind viciously shook the casements and hurled itself down the steep road to the swirl of waters. A moment's interlude of silence followed. Mary seized it.

'He's gone,' she told him, the repressed breath almost stifling her. 'I'm a free woman, Martin.'

'You—believe it?'

'I do.' The quiet in her eyes made her appear more than human. The light in the eerie room began to fade. Martin noticed it with sudden alarm.

'The light!' he said, hysterically. 'For God's sake, Mary, see to the lamp. Keep it burning, or I'll go mad.'

'I'll get more oil from the scullery,' Mary said, quietly, her fingers touching his face and steadying his quivering nerves. It was then she looked towards the chair. What she saw made her go forward quickly—Martin holding to her desperately. She touched the flesh of the upturned face. It was cold and like wax. She pushed Martin back.

'You were right, Martin,' she said. 'They *were* one.'

'D-dead?' quivered Martin.

She nodded. 'Both dead . . .'

He stood petrified, the fear frozen on his face as if it were the work of a ruthless and embittered artist. The rain pattered deafeningly on the room. She gathered him to her in the blackening shadows and coaxed the life and blood back to his features.

'Dead . . . dead . . . the five of them,' he kept muttering. 'And I'm alive. . . . They hated me . . . I know they hate me still, wherever they are. . . . If they could come here, they would—would——' His voice rose into hysteria in unison with the shrieking of the storm outside. Her voice, coaxing and calming him, was like a white feather floating in a fury of sound.

'You must hold on to yourself firmly,' she kept saying. 'We have won, we two, and we must not be cheated. Wait now till I get more oil from the scullery, and then you'll feel better.'

She settled him solicitously in a chair with his back to the dead man, and then stumbled over and through the slithering shadows into the scullery at the other end of the kitchen. He looked after her—glimpsed her undaunted head, and worshipped her. How brave she was! She was as brave and steady and as quiet as the light men kept burning above Orme Point. She would be the mother of his sons. . . . He glanced fearfully at the inert figure, as if expecting a thunderous protest. The light grew dimmer and dimmer. A long shadow passed from the dead man to himself, saluted him with mock gravity and scurried into a coil of ropes in a corner. His half-crazed mind followed it, and was winding the coils round the slippery sides of the shadow, when the wind with an unearthly shriek flung wide the heavy door and raced round and round the gloomy entrance as if it were a host of crazy human creatures, babbling, raving, cursing, and expectorating.

Martin jumped from the chair and cried. But the cry did not come. He fell to a sudden childish whimpering—his eyes staring and blurred by the strain of his fear. Small, darting streaks of light rent the shadowy tumult, and his distracted mind translated them as inexorable fingers beckoning to him.

'No, no, no . . .' he cried piteously. 'I can't, I can't . . . It's

too—terrible ... awful ... awful ... Oh, Mary, I'm lost!
They've come for me—the five of them ... I knew it ... I
knew it ...'

But the babbling grew louder, and the fingers still
beckoned. Outside the furies raged.

'Mary,' he sobbed, but the sob choked the strength of his
cry, and what did escape was swept away and tormented. His
fear and terror now possessed his whole being. Compelled by
the merciless fingers, he moved a step towards the door, two
steps, three steps ... He would have fallen down into unconsciousness could he have taken his eyes from the curving
fingers, but they held his gaze as if in some horrible vice, and
the babbling screamed and howled about his ears.

' Have mercy on me, have mercy on me,' he kept whimpering, as he was impelled forward. 'I'm not like you ... I have
never been strong. I can't look on terrible things ...'

It was then the fingers seemed to touch him, and the
babbling assaulted all his senses, like rowdy men met for sum-
mary justice. He felt himself being hurried past the crazy door,
and out into a black cavern of outraged and ravaged sensitive
things. A vicious blast of rain blinded him. Something
invisible that whirled and eddied hurled him forward. He saw
the beckoning fingers again on the edge of the cliff ... Then
suddenly he became aware of a new force that panted and was
brimful of tenacious energy. It flung itself upon him and bore
him down to the ground. He was dimly conscious that it was
dragging him over the wet earth, and that it was soft to the
touch and yet radiated strength. In his first coherent moment
he heard the clang of the heavy door and the clamour of the
disappointed babbling against it. He knew then that Mary
was with him and that her warm body encircled his own. He
could hear the violent pant of her breath, and when he looked
up her face was flushed and her eyes victorious.

'Stay in close to me,' he heard her say. 'Away in there. Don't
look out there or anywhere. Look only at me—at my eyes.'

He looked, and saw her heavy lashes and underneath
quietening pools of light, untormented by shadow or wind-

gust. He thought again of the quiet bright light above Orme Point. A great sob shook him and ran from his body into hers, making her a partaker of his humanity and his ignobility alike.

'Hold me in close to you, Mary,' he entreated her, 'and never let me go from you.'

Sitting on the damp, shadowy floor she drew his weakling head into her breast and suffered it. Once she glanced at the chair by the fireplace. The form on it still lay inert and grey, but to her it had no significance. To her, and such as her, the dead must be always meaningless.

Ultimately, a watery dawn came forth out of the grey waters. She looked down at the sleeping face and whispered some little thing that perhaps has no meaning in the dictionary of words. She lifted her head to the sorrowing daylight. The dawn is a sad woman, and for a moment they regarded each other—two women who must be about their business. She smiled slightly and, as if in answer, a single shaft of sunlight touched her tossed hair and made it beautiful.

ANTONIA WHITE

THE MOMENT OF TRUTH

O<small>N</small> the stone floor inlaid with coats of arms, only a few couples were dancing, yet the hall was filled with the lisping of feet. The music was as insistent as the band striking up when a man falls from a trapeze.

'Hardly anyone is dancing,' said Charlotte to the unknown man beside her, 'yet whenever I put out my hand, I touch someone.' But the stranger seemed not to have heard her. All his attention was taken up with the piece of string which he was twisting into elaborate bends. At first she was hurt because he was ignoring her. Then she realized that he was telling her something by means of the string. She tried to read words in the loops and twists. He tied a slip-knot and drew the noose over one finger. 'Is that——?' she began, and checked herself. For she had made an absurd mistake. The man beside her was not a stranger, but her husband, Richard.

And was she after all at Faringay? There was something not quite right about the hall. Looking up, she read the motto on one of the dark arches, 'Ne crede Byron'. The arch: the gilt letters were just as she remembered them, but the words should have been 'Labor ipse voluptas'.

She must keep quiet, ask no questions, draw attention to nothing, least of all to herself. Now the hall was entirely empty of dancers. But though the band brayed like a steam organ, she could still hear the whispering feet. There was no longer anyone near her, but a woman laughed close by her ear and an invisible skirt brushed her knee.

With every second the danger was growing. Looking for a way of escape, Charlotte noticed a door she had never seen before. Printed on it in large Gothic letters was the word MURDER.

Now she knew that she could not be too careful. She must act very quietly, very normally. She walked over towards the buffet, feeling her way through the unseen dancers. They would not make room for her but pressed against her, jostling and holding her back. She dared not wince or cry out, though she could feel hands passing up and down her spine, pinching her arms, stroking her throat. An invisible man embraced her, pushing his thighs against hers. A finger was thrust in her eye. A woman's bracelet caught in her hair. But, keeping back her terror, she went on slowly making her way through the crowd of laughing enemies.

By the buffet the space was clear. The man in the white cap carving a ham with a long thin knife raised his head and looked at her with eyes bolting from a doll's face. He leant over the table, and ran the knife blade caressingly down her arm. 'I *know*,' he whispered. It had come. She must get out. In a second it would be too late.

'Richard! Richard! Richard!' she screamed from bursting lungs.

The cry Charlotte heard as she broke through to the safer world was the thinnest wail, less audible than the pounding of her heart. She put out her hand to touch Richard and her knuckles encountered only wood. She seemed to be lying in a coffin that heaved under her with a shuddering creak. Was she awake or had she struggled out of one nightmare into another? She forced her eyes wide open and took deep gasps of breath. The air, smelling of oil and paint, was suffocating but it was the air of the tangible world. Groping along the ledge she found a switch and turned on the dim cabin light.

'Richard,' she said.

There was no answer.

Leaning over the edge of the bunk, she listened for his breathing. She heard nothing but the straining creak of the ship and the crash of the waves against the porthole. His dressing-gown swung towards her from the opposite wall and stayed suspended at a wide angle till the wall swung forward to meet it. The wall itself swerved from the straight and the dressing-gown lapsed back on to it. She stared at it as it swayed, hung suspended and dropped until she began to feel its sickening rhythm behind her eyes and had to look away.

At last she made herself climb down and peer into the lower bunk. The sheets were folded with the precision of a hospital bed. On the pillow lay nothing but Richard's watch. She picked it up, looked at the time, and crouched back on the bunk, dangling the watch by its strap. It was half-past one; more than two hours since he had kissed her good night and gone up on deck. Why had he left her for so long?

Ever since she had begun, a few months before, to have oppressive dreams, she counted on finding him near her when she fought out of them, always calling his name. He had learnt to slip an arm round her, even to mutter reassuring words, without waking from his sleep. Now that he was not there when she needed him such bitterness rose up in her that she could feel an acrid taste in her mouth.

The next lurch of the narrow cabin flung his dressing-gown against her knee. Snatching it from the hook, she huddled into it, meaning to go up on deck and find him. But she felt sick. Her knees bent under her and she dropped back, stooping, on the bunk.

The cabin was growing smaller, hotter, more imprisoning every minute. She seemed to have swollen to enormous size. The heavy man's dressing-gown was stifling her but she could not make the effort to take it off. Her skin pricked as if hairs were starting out of it. The bitterness vanished in the beginning of a terror worse than the nightmare, the waking terror from which there was no escape. She could neither bear to be alone in this dim, lurching cupboard nor get up strength to burst open the door. With eyes stiffening in their sockets, she could only crouch there, gripping the watch-strap as if it were a lifeline.

Trying to keep the fear from closing in on her, she focused all her mind on the watch. To her it was part of Richard's body. The silver back was stained from four years' contact with his flesh. It had marked him too, printing its shape in a white fetter on his wrist. Night after night the beat of its tiny metal pulse had sounded like a second heart, a fraction of him that remained awake while he slept. It had become so intimately his that, fingering it in his absence, she seemed to be touching something to which she had no right.

She had not held it in her hand since she had taken it shining from its case and given it him the night before they were married. The next morning, just as she was leaving her room to go across to the church where his father was waiting to marry them, he had run into her, breathless and laughing.

'My watch, Charlotte! I can't be married without my watch! I've raced back from the altar for it.'

She remembered how he looked, bright-eyed and ruddy from the November wind, his hair sleeked, a flower in his coat —the picture of a bridegroom.

But try as she would to hold the image, the tide of panic went on rising, sweeping her back from the real world. The watch slipped to the floor. She dropped back on the bunk with closed eyes and gasping mouth like a drowning woman beaten off from a lifeboat.

'Charlotte!'

His voice called her back. It sounded in the core of her ear, yet it seemed to come from another dimension like the voice of the nurse to which one wakes after chloroform. She forced up her eyelids and looked at him. He filled the cabin, standing over her in his loose oilskin coat.

'Charlotte, dear, are you awake or asleep?'

With a huge effort she made herself open her mouth and speak, only to say in a dry whisper:

'Your watch. On the floor. Don't tread on it.'

He picked up the watch. His face, as it stooped to the level of hers, still glistened with spray, and his hair was damp and ruffled.

'What is the matter, Charlotte? Are you ill?'

'I had a bad dream,' she said, staring past him.

'And I wasn't there. I'm sorry.'

'What does it matter?'

'Oh, Charlotte, not that voice. And why look at me as if I were an enemy?'

'Not an enemy. A stranger,' she said wearily.

'I shouldn't have stayed away so long.'

There was regret in his tone, not the mechanical gentleness she had lately come to expect. It softened the shell of her hatred. She sat up and let him put his arm round her shoulder. Sitting side by side, their heads leaning together, their foreheads drooped, they seemed to be mourning a common loss.

'What was your dream, Charlotte?'

'I woke before it became too bad. It was about Faringay.'

'You are haunted by that house. Why do you keep dreaming about the past?'

'I can't inhabit the present any more.'

His arm tightened as the ship gave a lurch.

'We shouldn't be talking so late. We may be keeping people awake in the next cabin.'

She drew away from him in anger. Then she laughed.

'You inhabit the present all right.'

'It makes you so angry that I do. Yet one of us must.'

'Perhaps one is enough,' she said almost gaily.

He stood up and tried gently to draw her to her feet. But she shook her head and settled back on the bunk. He loomed above her, balancing on his strong legs, adjusting them to the movement of the ship.

'Don't you ever have dreams, Richard?'

'Mine don't make stories like yours.'

'Do you never have a dream that seems more true than life? That shows you something you never knew before—or were afraid to know?'

He began to wind his watch.

'Sometimes, perhaps.'

'You don't tell me them.'

She glanced up and saw his face set and heavy. In the dim light the shadows under his eyes were dark as bruises. She knew he was tired out but she hardened to him.

'I don't always dream of the past, Richard.'

He went on turning the knob of his watch.

'You'll break the mainspring,' she cried in a burst of rage. Then, bitterly, 'I forgot. You'd never ill-treat a piece of *machinery*, would you?'

He laid the watch down carefully and took her by the wrist, pressing his fingers on it as if feeling her pulse.

'Charlotte!' he said quietly and urgently, 'Charlotte! You must get some sleep now.'

He pulled her up against the dead weight of her resistance.

'I'll help you into your bunk.'

'No. I feel sick.'

'You'll be better lying flat. It's beginning to calm down. Up on deck I could hardly keep my legs.'

'Then why did you stay so long?'

He kissed her forehead.

'Up you go. Carefully.'

As she scrambled up clumsily, a sudden roll shot her forehead against an iron staple and Richard cried out.

'You needn't pity me about physical pain,' she said. 'It's a relief.'

'You don't want that heavy old dressing-gown. You'll be far too hot.'

She took it off and let it fall.

'I don't remember putting it on. I must be a little crazy.'

He smoothed her pillow, pulled the harsh sheets over her and putting back her tangled hair, began to stroke her forehead. For a minute she lay with closed eyes, not resisting him. A tear oozed under her eyelid and crawled down her temple.

'Will you sleep now?' he said softly.

Her eyes sprang open.

'You say I always dream of the past. What about my other dream? The one about your leaving me?'

'You've dreamt that ever since we married, haven't you?' he said in his same soft voice, still stroking her head. She jerked it away from his touch.

'I shall go on dreaming it. Until it comes true.'

'Has it ever been near coming true?'

'How should I know?' She closed her eyes once more. A wave exploded with a gentle crash against the porthole.

'If only we could open it and get some air,' said Richard.

Though Charlotte had withdrawn too far into herself to care about the heat or the reek of oil, she knew how they must sicken his wind-freshened senses. Yet she beat her fist against the ledge of the bunk, crying:

'You mean I am stifling you. Go on. Say it. Say it.'

'I will say nothing of the kind,' he whispered in patient fury. She bared her teeth and tried to strike him, but he leaned over her pinioning her shoulders like a lover or a murderer. She lay helpless for a moment, gasping with anger. Then suddenly she smiled.

'Why do I have to behave like this? Why can't you stop me?'

He smiled too and shook his head.

'Let me go now,' she said, speaking for the first time in her normal voice. 'You needn't hold me down. I am not dangerous.'

He took his hands from her shoulders and began to stroke her arm as if he were expertly and mechanically stroking an animal.

'I know,' he said.

She lay with closed eyes, quiet but unappeased. There was something she wanted to tell him, something urgent which kept flitting just out of reach of her thought like a forgotten name. He kissed her lightly and began, quietly as a thief, to lower himself into his own bunk. When she remembered what she had been groping for and softly called his name, he did not answer.

Their bedroom in the Hotel Berrichon was square and low-ceilinged, with a floor of red tiles arranged in a honeycomb pattern. Stiff yellow lace curtains were looped back from the window that looked out over the whole expanse of the Baie de la Fresnaye. Madame Berrichon leered at Richard and Charlotte as she patted the red eiderdown of the enormous bed.

'You will hardly find a bed so comfortable in the whole of Brittany. My neighbours are satisfied with the old-fashioned *lits clos*—mere cupboards. But I am from Paris. I am civilized. I do not look on a bed as something in which one huddles one-self to sleep like an animal. In Paris we say that the bed is the battlefield of love.'

'Indeed,' said Richard, politely. Charlotte turned away with a sigh of exasperation and began to pour water from the tiny cracked pitcher into the basin.

'Madame is annoyed?' said Madame Berrichon, in her hoarse purring contralto. 'One does not say such things to English ladies? Forgive me. I am a person of impulses. I do not weigh my words.'

'Are we the only people staying here?' asked Richard.

'Yes, monsieur. It is early in the season. And in any case few people care for a place so remote. Only those who wish to be alone with nature—or painters—or——' she lowered her heavy wrinkled lids, 'lovers.'

'We only found it by accident,' Richard said, with an uneasy glance at Charlotte's back. 'We set out from St. Malo this morning and we've been driving all day. My wife is very tired.'

'Believe me, it was no accident,' said Madame Berrichon. She faced him squarely, a solid shapeless figure in her dark shawl and black calico skirt. A shaft from the setting sun struck her face like limelight, showing up the black down on her upper lip and the open pores of her yellow skin. 'Nothing happens by accident in this life. I had an intuition that you would come—so strong that I sent my husband into Matignon to buy langoustes and other good things. He will tell you my intuitions are always justified.'

'I am sure they are, madame,' said Richard, meeting her eyes with a stare of polite impertinence.

'You laugh. You think I am a foolish old woman,' she said with dignity. 'It is true I do not concoct verses, only good dishes. But at heart, monsieur, I am a poet. And whether you believe me or not, I am in touch with the most subtle forces of nature. I know by a certainty I cannot describe—a magnetic current in my blood perhaps—that you were both sent here for a purpose. And if you do not know it, madame your wife knows it, though she pretends not to listen to me.'

Charlotte did not speak or turn round until Madame Berrichon had glided out of the room, moving heavily yet swiftly over the tiles in her felt slippers.

'She's right. We can't get away even if we want to. She's a spider—a witch.'

'Well, she's got an ideal web or castle. It's an old sea-mill, she told me. Built right out into an arm of the bay. When the tide's up, there's water on three sides of the house.'

'In fact we are really prisoners,' said Charlotte.

'You forget there's a fourth side. Stop thinking about Madame Berrichon and come and look out of the window.'

'I'm frightened of that old woman,' said Charlotte, moving slowly up to where Richard stood by the window.

'You should paint her and get her out of your system. You could do a wonderful portrait of her—a cross between a Balzac concierge and the Delphic sibyl.'

'I shall never paint again,' said Charlotte gloomily. 'I can't see outside things any more. Only beastly things in my own mind.'

He drew her arm through his with a brotherly gesture.

'All the same, come and look out of the window.'

They leant together on the low narrow sill.

'You could dive straight out of the window into the sea,' she said.

'You'd better not try. See those dark patches under the surface? Rocks—jagged rocks too. You wouldn't have a chance.'

'What's happened to the sun? A few minutes ago there was a blazing sunset. Now look.'

The sky was overdrawn with fine cloud like a fog in the upper air. After the windless heat of the day, a breeze sprang up from nowhere, fanning gusts of invisible rain as fine as dust in their parched faces.

'Perhaps the wind and the rain come up with the tide,' said Richard. 'Can't you feel it's only on the surface? Underneath the air is still as hot and solid as ever. You can almost see the rain turning into steam.'

'How deep is the water?'

'Twenty or thirty feet I should say. Probably we're left high and dry when the tide goes out. Just rocks and mud.'

'What are those birds, Richard? The white ones. They're not ordinary gulls.'

Between the grey sky and the olive-green sea white birds skimmed to and fro, a few feet above the surface, their black heads bent towards the water. Every now and then they dropped like stones into the sea, then flashed up again in an arrowy curve. Richard waited till one settled on an old boat moored to a ring in the wall.

'Look! do you see his forked tail? They're sea swallows: you can't see the fork when they fly—they move so fast—the feathers all whirl together.'

'Like spun glass: like the birds with spun-glass tails we had on the Christmas tree.'

For a moment Charlotte forgot everything in the pleasure of watching the shooting, diving swallows. Then she turned from the window with a sigh.

'I wish I were a bird. Or even a rock or a patch of seaweed. Anything—anything but a human being.'

She went to the basin and began to wash her hands. Richard threw himself on the bed.

'Is that water warm?'

'No. It's icy—like mountain water.'

He yawned. 'Then I can't shave. You'll have to put up with me with a beard.'

'You can't look worse than I do,' said Charlotte, peering at herself in a greenish speckled mirror. Suddenly she turned and faced him.

'Richard, why didn't you tell me?'

'Tell you what?' he said, in a voice lazy, yet guarded.

'That I've suddenly aged ten years.'

'Don't talk nonsense.'

'You're not looking at me.'

'I don't have to. There's nothing the matter with your face. It's that absurd glass.'

'The glass can't give me those lines. Or those shadows under my eyes.'

'Then it's the way the light falls. Stop being morbid.'

Her face was strained and searching.

'Richard! seriously, I *do* look terrible, don't I?'

He smiled at the ceiling.

'Of course you look a little tired. Who wouldn't, after that night on the boat and driving all day in the sun and dust? Two nights' rest and you'll look wonderful.'

She turned her back on him again, fiercely dragging a comb through her soft fair hair that had gone limp from the heat.

'I hate my face,' she muttered: 'hate it! hate it! hate it!'

'Well, I don't,' he said good-humouredly. He swung himself off the bed and stood up, stretching his firm handsome brown arms. 'Come down and have a drink. We both need one.'

The dining-room was large and dim, lit only by three small windows on the landward side. It was paved with the same dull red honeycomb tiles as the bedroom and furnished only with two dark presses and a dozen tables covered with red and white oilcloth. At the far end, like a huge well-head filled with stones, the shaft which had once held the hoppers of the mill thrust up through the floor. Underneath, though muffled by the stones, the tide could be heard gurgling in the empty shaft.

They sat down at the only table that was laid. Through the window they could see a small, dusty courtyard with a battered table, a few iron chairs, and a fig tree. A yellow mongrel was asleep on one of the chairs; at the table sat Monsieur Berrichon, a wizened little man in a beret and a faded blue blouse, sipping a glass of wine, round which the wasps hovered and buzzed.

Beside Charlotte's plate lay a passion-flower, a star of thick green-white petals with a fringe of blue rays. From the centre of the star four dark stamens stood up, lined with bright yellow pollen and three curious bosses like nail heads. She picked it up and sniffed its strong fleshy scent.

'How did this come here? It couldn't be you, Richard?'

He smiled and shook his head.

Madame Berrichon's felt slippers shuffled on the tiles behind her. Charlotte dropped the flower and turned to find the old woman at her elbow, holding out in both hands an enormous knobbed red sea-spider. The creature's body was larger than a crab; its long spiky arms waved viciously and helplessly trying to clutch the black shawl.

'You see, madame? I could not resist proving to you that we expected you. Tonight I can only give you a simple meal—but tomorrow, a little feast.'

Charlotte drew back from the waving, clutching tentacles.

'Aha! you are nervous? He is a wicked fellow, no? He would like to crush your hand with those pincers—but we are Christians, are we not? We repay evil with good. I have the water already boiling in my kitchen to give him a nice hot bath.'

'Please take it away,' said Charlotte, shuddering.

'Madame is too sensitive,' said Madame Berrichon, winking at Richard. 'I sympathize. I am sensitive myself—to a degree you would not understand. But one must be a realist too. Providence has arranged that many things should only be good and useful when they are dead.'

She retreated slowly to the kitchen, still talking half-threateningly, half-amorously to the sea-spider.

'Do you think it was she who put the passion-flower there?' asked Charlotte, when the kitchen door closed behind Madame Berrichon.

'She's quite capable of it.'

Charlotte pushed the flower away from her.

Louison, Madame's rosy-cheeked, eighteen-year-old niece, in her blue apron and sabots, trotted in with their soup. She glanced at the passion-flower and flushed.

'Madame is offended that I put this flower on the table?'

'Oh, was it you, Louison?' Charlotte drew it back to her. 'No, I love it. I was showing it to my husband.'

She felt herself blushing in her turn.

'But you see, Louison, I can't wear it, I haven't a pin.'

The girl took a pin from her apron and fastened the flower to Charlotte's dress. They both smiled.

'There, madame. Now you look like a bride.'

Blushing again and glancing at Richard under her fingers, Louison picked up her tray and trotted off again, her sabots pattering like hooves on the tiles.

'There—you see,' said Richard triumphantly. 'It's not all black magic here.'

Charlotte fingered the flower, feeling suddenly old and exhausted.

'She's charming. All the same, it's a little ironical to be treated like a bride.'

As she drooped, Richard seemed to revive. His eyes widened and shone as he filled their glasses with the cheap red wine.

'Drink up,' he said, looking aggressively young and healthy. 'Here's to your getting better.'

Charlotte drank too.

'A thoroughly sensible, practical wish. If Louison heard it, that would be the end of her honeymoon illusions.'

'Charlotte, you know as well as I do that nothing can go right for us till you're cured.'

'Cured of what? There's nothing the matter with me.'

'I wish that were true.'

'Then act as if it were,' she said recklessly. 'You treat me as if I were sick or mad, and I become sick and mad. It's your fault.'

He opened his mouth as if he were going to speak. Instead, he finished his glass and filled it up again.

'Perhaps the only thing that's really wrong with us, Charlotte, is that we don't drink enough.'

'Maybe it's as simple as that. You always used to say you hated drink.'

'I've said a lot of idiotic things.'

Charlotte stared at him. His face, which she was accustomed to seeing gentle, controlled, almost too anxious to please, looked defiant, even a little dissolute.

'Richard, you're different in some way.'

'Well, shouldn't one be different on a holiday? Or perhaps you haven't seen me for so long you've forgotten what I'm like?'

'Nearly six weeks. We've never been apart so long before.'

'No.'

'It's supposed to be a good thing for people who are married, isn't it?'

For no reason—or perhaps because of the wine—she suddenly began to feel confident, almost exultant.

'I'm sure it's an *excellent* thing,' she said emphatically.

'Is it?' He sipped his drink, frowning.

'I've been such a *fool*, Richard.' She took a deep gulp of the harsh wine. 'Working myself up into such a state over nothing. But I can be different too, you'll see.'

'You couldn't help being ill.'

It was again the voice she dreaded; gentle, reasonable, placating. But she could ignore it.

'I'm not ill, I tell you. I've just been giving way to myself. Illusion, nothing but illusion. But everything's going to be all right now. Don't I look different already?'

She smiled theatrically, feeling the flesh stretched and tingling over her cheekbones.

'You look splendid. All the same, you must take things quietly for a bit.'

She made a face.

'You're worse than the doctors.'

'You always rush things so. I get giddy trying to keep up with you.'

'I'd like to get the car out and drive for miles. Let's get away from the old witch and her mill.'

'Wait until tomorrow. You don't know how tired you are.'

She put down her glass and sighed.

'It's no good. I believe you want to depress me. You want me to be wretched, So that everyone can pity you and say what a wonderful husband you are to that tiresome woman.'

'Don't talk nonsense,' he said, gently.

'We're never in the same mood at the same moment. Why is it? A moment ago, you were gay and I felt flat. Now I'm gay, and you're wilting before my eyes; is it the same with all married people?'

'I don't know: I daresay.' He lit a cigarette. 'Is there anything you'd like to do?'

She smoked for a minute or two, greedily and mechanically, scattering ash on the oilcloth.

'No, nothing. You make me feel there's no point in doing anything.'

'I'm not much good to you, am I, Charlotte?'

He swept up the ash she had dropped into a neat little heap.

'You're too good, that's just the trouble. Too patient, too considerate. Everything I do irritates you; even the way I smoke a cigarette.'

'Oh, I can put up with that,' he laughed. 'My tidiness is a vice; something you have to put up with.'

'If you only had one grain of viciousness or disorderliness.'

He blew the little heap of ashes on to the floor.

'You know me through and through, don't you? No wonder you find me so dull.'

'I don't know you,' she said thoughtfully. 'I only know what you say and do.'

'Isn't that enough? The trouble is I'm too simple for you.'

'You're not simple: you're not simple at all,' she sighed. 'Or am I the only woman incapable of understanding you?'

'You've such an itch for understanding things, haven't you? Why can't you accept me as I am?'

'I do more than accept you,' she said quietly. 'I love you.'

He looked down, avoiding her eyes, his face heavy and clouded.

'Yes, I suppose you feel that is more.'

Her throat went dry.

'You don't want to love me. Is that it? Does that mean——?'

He would not let her finish. 'Don't let's discuss what words mean. I tell you we won't get anywhere with words.'

'Why not, with the right words?' she insisted obstinately.

He jerked his head like a horse on a too short rein.

'I tell you I haven't your idolatrous respect for words.'

'Yet you're so careful with them. You never exaggerate as I do. Never say more than you mean.'

He smiled. She noticed again how tight-lipped and secret his mouth was in contrast to the almost aggressive frankness of the eyes. The lips always looked bruised and chafed as if they were made of older, more worn material than the fresh skin of his face.

'I expect it's just part of the tidiness that infuriates you so.'

'At any rate you're honest. I cling to that.'

'Poor Charlotte. It's a negative thing to cling to.'

'It's enough,' she boasted, knowing that she lied.

Charlotte lay back in the great bed watching Richard moving about the room, unpacking her suitcase and folding her clothes.

'Why don't you let me do anything for myself tonight?' she said.

'You're tired.'

'But it could all wait till tomorrow.'

He smiled and went on inexorably arranging everything in perfect order. When everything was in place, he spread his heavy dressing-gown over her feet.

'You'll be cold in that great icy bed.'

'But aren't you coming to bed yourself?'

'Very soon. I'm going to take a turn outside first.'

Her face stiffened with disappointment as she watched him slipping a jacket over his short-sleeved shirt.

'Just as you like,' she said listlessly.

'Don't be angry, Charlotte. You know what a fool I am about strange places. I can't settle down till I've got my bearings.'

She managed to smile. 'Then of course you must go.'

'You can be an angel when you want to.'

She laughed, pleased at having controlled herself.

'You're thinking, why can't I always be?'

'Yes, why can't you?' he mocked.

'I'll tell you,' she said, sliding her fingers under the cuff of his jacket and stroking his bare wrist. 'It wears one down, being married to a man who always gives such excellent reasons for everything he does.'

He kissed her hand, disengaged himself gently and went out, closing the door stealthily as if she were already asleep.

But she was no longer sleepy. Fighting down an impulse to call him back, she sat up in bed, clenching her hands round her knees and staring in front of her. Because it was not yet quite dark outside, she felt like a child sent to bed for punishment. She got up and padded round the room; the cold slippery tiles were ice to her bare feet. The mantelpiece distracted her for a few minutes with its load of photographs, oleographs of the Sacred Heart and the Little Flower, black-framed memorial cards, and brass vases filled with immortelles, all set out with precision like the ornaments of an altar on a starched cloth edged with crochet lace. She examined the photographs with interest, recognizing Madame in a wedding group, Louison in the long white dress and veil of a First Communicant, Monsieur Berrichon, twenty years younger, in an ill-fitting army uniform. But these were quickly exhausted. How was she to kill time till Richard came back? She could not lie in the cold bed staring and thinking. In the last months she had become afraid to think. Her very thoughts were tarnished. They split and unravelled into meaningless ends. Often she believed she was going insane. Something inside her seemed to have died and to be filling her mind, even her body, with corruption. Now it was as if she had accidentally overheard a terrible secret and that everything she did or thought was an attempt to stop her ears and forget. At other times she was like a person who must guess an impossible riddle on pain of death and who has only a few hours left in which to find the answer. Outwardly her life went on as before, except that for some months she had been growing languid, irritable and prone to dreams which oppressed her for days.

She had come away for this holiday determined to shake off the shadow. With all his vigorous sanity, Richard himself had lately begun to look moody and careworn. She guessed it was for his sake as much as hers that he had made her give up work for a time and go away alone to the country. It had been dull misery being away from him, yet now that she saw him again she felt more shut away than ever, as a drowning man feels his isolation more bitterly when he can see people walking on the shore. There were moments when she hated him, but they were nothing to the loathing she felt for herself. Yet even her self-hatred was not pure; it had an element of gloating in it; a strain of vile pleasure, as well as disgust.

Tonight, she told herself, she would not give way to it. Already she could feel herself slipping. When Richard came back there must not be a repetition of the night on the boat. What could she do to pass the time in a sane, normal way until she felt safe enough to put out the light? She remembered that there was a detective story in the pocket of the coat Richard had worn on the journey. She opened the door of the cupboard and saw the coat hanging inside. The green and white cover of the book showed over the top of the pocket. As she pulled it out a letter fell out with it. It was a thick letter in a blue envelope, unopened. She picked it up and stared at it, for she knew the writing. Her immediate thought was 'This is really meant for me'. The conviction was so strong that she was on the point of opening it though it was clearly addressed to 'Richard Crane'. She glared again at the envelope as if by doing so she could change what was written on it. Then she saw it was not addressed to their London house, but to a poste restante near Waterloo. The shock was so great that she felt nothing but a mild exhilaration. The exhilaration had nothing to do with her mind, which remained perfectly blank; it was altogether physical, as if she had drunk something warm and stimulating.

There was a knock at the door. Thinking it was Richard, she slipped the letter into the coat pocket and darted back into bed, pulling the sheets up to her chin. She could feel that her eyes were shining and her face set in a mask of bright expectancy as she called out 'Come in'.

It was Madame Berrichon, carrying a steaming glass on a saucer with the air of a priestess carrying a sacred vessel.

'I had a little conversation with Monsieur your husband,' she said, as she majestically approached the bed. 'It appears you have been indisposed, madame, and have bad nights. I have taken the liberty of bringing you something to make you sleep.'

A thought flashed up in Charlotte's mind; a thought so fantastic that she did not attempt to brush it away. 'He has sent this woman to poison me.'

Out loud she said politely: 'It is kind of you, madame, but drugs don't have the effect on me. I sleep better without them.'

'This is no drug, madame. I myself abominate drugs. It is a tisane made of wholesome natural substances, a distillation of passion-flowers, to be exact.'

She glanced at the passion-flower, wilting in a glass on the chest-of-drawers.

'A charming flower, no? Alive it gives us pleasure; dead it gives us peace.'

'My husband made a mistake, Madame Berrichon. There is nothing the matter with me.'

Madame Berrichon stooped and brought her face close to Charlotte's, fixing her with huge eyes, the colour of black coffee.

'I do not need to be told you are ill,' she said, in her hoarse purr. 'I do not judge as doctors. I judge from deeper sources. And I tell you are not only ill, but in grave danger.'

'Nonsense,' said Charlotte, wishing she could laugh, yet feeling her throat contract. 'You are trying to frighten me. Why?'

'Certainly not, madame. I am speaking only for your good. How do I know? Because Providence has given me a nature of extraordinary sensibility. And I pay a price for it. When others suffer, I suffer in every fibre of my being. Tonight you will sleep, but I, I shall not close my eyes.'

'You are too sensitive, madame,' said Charlotte coldly, remembering the sea-spider.

'Sensitive, madame, that is too banal a word. Good Catholic as I am, I dare not go to Mass. The chanting disturbs my nerves too much.' She turned up her eyes till only half the iris showed in the blood-shot yellowish whites. 'Believe me, madame, I have only to see my Piboulette with her ducklings, to think of my dog Nanasse, to weep like a child.'

Madame Berrichon brought her eyes into focus again and thrust the glass into Charlotte's limp hand.

'You must drink, madame. Before it gets cold.'

Powerless, only wanting to be rid of the woman, Charlotte took a sip of a hot liquid, bitter as alum.

Madame Berrichon watched her greedily, anchoring her hands to her solid hips.

'A trifle bitter? There are many bitter things in life as you, madame, are still too young to know. But this bitterness brings sweetness. When you have drained every drop—piff, paff—you will be in the arms of Morpheus. So deeply asleep that your charming husband on his return might suppose you dead. So, another little, little sip.'

On a sudden impulsion Charlotte launched the glass through the open window. It fell with a faint splash into the sea.

'Softly, madame,' said the woman without moving. She gave an imperturbable, pitying leer. 'You see, I am not angry. With hysterics, one must be patient.'

'I am not an hysteric,' Charlotte muttered between her teeth.

'Quite so, quite so, my poor little lady,' the other purred. 'What more natural? So handsome a husband—of course one would not wish him to find one asleep. So very sound asleep too.'

Charlotte felt locked as if in one of her nightmares. She bit her lips so as not to scream for Richard. She looked wildly round the room, staring imploringly at each object he had so carefully arranged, his brushes, a jar of brilliantine, her own powder-bowl, as if they could exorcize this presence. But implacably her eyes were drawn back to Madame Berrichon's face.

'He is late, is he not, the charming husband?' said Madame Berrichon, moving away very slowly but still fixing her with the obscene eyes of a witch and a midwife.

She did not speak again until she reached the door.

'Believe me, madame, I do not hold your ingratitude against you. You are not responsible for your actions. I have done what I could. You prefer to reject it. I hope you will not suffer for it.'

She lingered a moment in the open door, like an actress leaving the stage.

'I too, madame, have a good husband.'

Then shrugging her black woollen shoulders, she added very softly with a cunning, confederate smile:

'All the same, my little lady, when I look for warmth, for understanding, for fidelity, I turn, not to any human being, but to Nanasse my dog.'

When Richard came back an hour later, he found Charlotte sitting bolt upright in bed, her hands knotted round her raised knees. She did not turn her head as he came in but glared straight in front of her with round glassy eyes. A bright blue woollen scarf sagging round her shoulders took all the colour from her face. She looked at once like a sick child and an immeasurably old woman.

'Charlotte', he said, feeling his heart contract with pity and terror. She did not speak or move. He took a step towards her.

'My dear, what is it? Are you ill? Have you had a dream?'

Still not looking at him, she spoke at last in a small, dry, high-pitched voice.

'Curious, aren't you? For such a *very* incurious chap.'

The pert words coming out of the stiff, livid face shocked him as if a corpse had begun to giggle. He sat down on the bed and taking her by both shoulders began to shake her.

'Charlotte, for God's sake.'

Her body rocked to and fro under his hands like a doll's. When he left off shaking her she went on in exactly the same tone.

'You might at least be decently polite to her. After all she is a friend of mine.'

Though he was in the direct line of her stare, he felt she could not see him.

'Charlotte,' he said quietly, 'can you hear me speaking?'

Her expression changed. She turned her head as if she expected to find him at her side.

'Yes,' she answered fretfully, 'of course I can hear you. What are you saying?'

Still quietly he went on.

'Now will you turn your head and look at *me*.'

There was a long pause before her head very slowly came round.

'And now, Charlotte, will you tell me what and who you are talking about?'

Her fine, almost invisible eyebrows went up. The eyes grew rounder still.

'Oh, *that*,' she said, like an impudent child. 'Didn't you know?'

'For Heaven's sake, stop this.' He crouched forward staring back at her like a hypnotist. Her eyes stayed blank and glassy; then a flicker of helpless terror came and went like the dart of a fin under ice.

'My dear, you *must* tell me. What is it I've done? Or that you imagine I've done.'

At last her eyelids relaxed. She tried to speak and could not, until she had passed her tongue two or three times over her dry lips.

'How do I know? I don't read letters.' She closed her eyes and added in a whisper, 'yet.'

He let out the breath he had been holding on a long sigh.

Sitting back on the bed, he took her hands in his. She struggled for a moment to tug them away, then let them lie cold and inert in his grip.

'Listen to me,' he said, 'you are torturing yourself in your imagination. About what?'

'You should know.' Her voice was reasonable but aloof.

'I will tell you what I think. You have found a letter written to me by'—he swallowed—'by someone we both know.'

'By Rachel Summerhill,' she said loudly.

'Mightn't there be a dozen explanations of that besides the one you're thinking of?'

'Even you can't invent a dozen reasons on the spur of the moment', she said, glib as an actress. He let go of her hands abruptly.

'All right, if you want a scene, we'll have a scene. God knows I ought to be good at them by now.' He stood up.

She clutched wildly at him.

'No Richard, no Richard': her face crumpled up. 'I'll behave myself. Only don't be angry, don't leave me alone.'

'I'm not going.'

She put her hands on her cheeks as if to hold the skin and muscles in place.

'It's the not knowing I can't stand. I don't care how bad it is. You must tell me.'

'Suppose there's nothing to tell?'

She examined him with an old, searching, impersonal gaze He gazed back at her unflinchingly.

'Your eyes never tell anything.'

'I'll answer any question you like.'

'Truthfully?'

'Yes. But, Charlotte, for both our sakes, think carefully before you ask.'

Suddenly she sighed, looking at him almost with friendliness.

'I wish I had no memory.'

'So do I.' He risked a faint smile.

She looked not at his face, but at the coat pocket over his heart.

'Rachel Summerhill. Somehow I didn't think she'd be the first. If she is the first.' She was silent for a minute. Then she began to mutter, like a child muttering to itself but meaning to be overheard. 'It doesn't make sense. I used to have to force him to stay in the days she came to see us. He said she was such a bore. What was it he called her? An American college virgin carrying the torch of knowledge on graduation day.'

He put his hand under her chin and lifted her head, gripping her jaw so firmly that she winced.

'Ask your questions. Or keep quiet,' he said roughly.

She wrenched her face away.

'Was it pleasant, making love with her? Who enjoyed it most, you or Rachel?'

In spite of himself, his hands flew up towards her neck. She gave a spurt of excited laughter.

'You don't have to answer now.'

But the words he was trying to keep back burst out, not through his throat, it seemed to him, but through his ribs. Automatically he put both hands on his chest as if to stop a flow of blood as he heard himself say:

'It was the only real thing that ever happened to either of us.'

Even then, Charlotte was so silent that for a whole minute he could believe he had not spoken and was merely watching words, written in smoke, fading on the air. He believed it until he looked at Charlotte's face and saw on it the same fear and exaltation he could feel on his own. For what seemed a long time they confronted each other, each searching the other's face like a mirror, in an intimacy of disaster.

A gust of wind blew out the stiff lace curtains at the window. Charlotte gave a long shuddering sigh like a person waking from an anaesthetic. Her calmed face suddenly decomposed. She flung herself on Richard, tearing at his coat, butting his chest with her head.

He did not resist, but let her hammer him with blind, childish blows. Her whole body shook with dry sobs of anger. Finally, weak and breathless, she stopped battering at him and tried to push him away. He remained immovable, secure in himself and strong enough to pity her.

Charlotte dropped back, exhausted, on the pillows. Then, staring at the ceiling, she began a long monotonous babble like the babble in delirium. At first he tried not to listen. Then in spite of himself he was sucked into these endless coils of words. She raved quietly on and on, not attacking him, but coldly, ferociously accusing herself. For long intervals she would show no consciousness of his being there, then she would implore him to go further away.

'It's not safe for anyone to come near me. You don't understand. I am poisoned, poisoned right through.'

He did not dare to deny or to interrupt. The terrible words multiplied and multiplied, till he seemed to be watching the multiplication, cell by cell, of a cancer. He clenched his hands till the nails were white. He longed, like a fish gasping for water, not for Rachel herself, but for the thought of Rachel, cool, limited, single. But the thought of her could no more form in his mind than a snowflake could form in a hot room. It seemed to him that for all eternity he would never see anything but the lace curtains, the naked electric light, the photographs, the harsh blue scarf, and Charlotte's distorted face. To shut them out, he hid his face in his hands. But he could not shut out the voice. It went on: a rise and fall of sound in which he no longer distinguished words.

Then abruptly, it stopped. Other different noises followed. They conveyed nothing to him. He did not look up. He could feel Charlotte was no longer there in the bed. But he could not look up. A long time seemed to pass. Then a rasping, metallic noise behind him made him start so violently that he thought he must have fallen asleep. Uncovering his face and jumping up he saw Charlotte at the wide-open window, carefully hoisting herself on to the ledge outside. In two steps he was behind her, holding her round the waist. She crouched down on the ledge and turned a blind, set face to him, not struggling, but resigning herself to his hold. They stood for a moment in a grotesque embrace; then, with the force of an uncoiling spring, Charlotte threw herself forward, nearly dragging him with her. Lurching half-over the sill he could see far below the dark masses of slippery, jagged rock, half-bared by the ebbing tide. He regained his balance and braced his knees, making his thighs and legs heavy. She was struggling now with unbelievable fury like a sail full of wind. His arms turned numb; his feet slithered on the floor but he still did not let go. Suddenly Charlotte seemed to dwindle to half her size. Turning, she slipped through his arms like a fish, and dropped down over the sill. For a second her white face hung suspended in the frame of the open window, then disappeared leaving only the two clinging hands. Richard reeled back, too weak to make any more effort.

The hands were relaxing their grip. They no longer seemed to have any connection with Charlotte. He found himself watching them impersonally, waiting for them to disappear. His head was beginning to clear. He drew a deep breath of the cold, sea air and felt deeply refreshed. Now his head was perfectly clear. It contained a single thought.

'I want her to die,' he said to himself.

In the overwhelming relief of acknowledging it his muscles suddenly asserted themselves and adjusted themselves with extraordinary skill. He made a dive forward from his hips, reached down, caught Charlotte under the armpits and dragged her up through the window. A tremendous wave of exultation in his own strength, in the exquisitely stressed and balanced movement he had just made went over him. The limp dead weight of her body as he pulled her in and held her against him, her feet dangling, seemed no more than the weight of a small animal. He lowered her gently till her feet touched the floor. She leant on him unresisting, her head against his shoulder.

Still with one arm round her he closed the window and pulled the curtains. Then he lifted her up, laid her on the bed, turned out the light and lay down beside her. She was still panting and shivering. He pulled his thick dressing-gown over them both and waited till her breathing was calm before he spoke. He was no longer frightened of anything he might say to her.

'Silly Charlotte. Why did you have to do that?'

She lay against him with an abandonment of trust he had never before felt in her.

'You wanted me dead,' she said peacefully.

He started, but she neither stiffened nor shrank away.

'You said so. Didn't you know?' Her voice was only a sleepy murmur.

He was too drunk with delicious torpor to answer. There was no more need for words; for the first time in their life together they were in complete accord. As they sank into the same profound sleep, they did not press closer, but their breathing gradually timed itself to the same rhythm till, at the vanishing point of consciousness, a single pulse seemed to beat through their two bodies.

MICHAEL SAYERS

THE JEW IN THE MOON

DEAR Fellows. I am mad? Believe me, all men are mad! This is the way it is: perhaps I am not so mad. Everybody can't fit in the lunatic asylums, can they? Only consider the expense! So what do they do, eh? All the mad people live in the world and the few ones with right heads they lock up in houses with walls round them. It is cheaper that way. . . .

I wouldn't complain if you could get a drop to drink now and then. Not at all. But can I help my taste? I like a drop of brandy, of whisky, of wine now and then. Am I a stone, or have I a tongue and a throat? And it's very cold in this place where I find myself. A man must have a drop to drink. It makes him feel good. Once upon a time there was a rabbi who liked it too, but people didn't think he ought to. 'Why do you drink, rabbi?' they kept saying. 'For why?' said the rabbi: 'because King Solomon was a wise man.' 'And what sort of answer is that?' said the people. 'King Solomon liked a drop now and then,' said the rabbi. 'How can you tell that?' said the people. 'How?' said the rabbi: 'because King Solomon was a wise man.'

That's the way it is, and we go here and we go there, and seek shadows and clutch bones. Men kill, steal, outrage. The Jews come and go from land to land over the whole world. Thousands of years, thousands of years, and the end is not yet. But the end will come. For what do we live, ah? For what do we grow and study and add cells to our brains? Is desolation to be the outcome? Never fear that. A strange change will happen in human hearts. Take my word for it. Yes, a strange change. . . .

Fellows, troubles are over. There is so much room on the moon, you would be surprised! It looks the size of a soup-plate, but it has sea and land, and cucumbers grow there, too. What more could a Jew want, eh? And if Cossacks come, and anti-semites, and pogromists, you say *Shoo! Shoo!* to them in a loud voice and they go away. Don't mind them who tell you that the flag of Israel won't fly in the cold air. Personally the Man in the Moon confided to me, privately, and he said: 'All Jews are welcome——'

Fellows, fellows, what a life I've had! Chaim Lucky One, they called me. God be thanked, I am lucky. I am alive. Leah is dead, Isaac is dead; I am alive. Eh, my wife, my Leah! A tiger, a bear, a leopard in the jungle would not have done it. Where is the humanity? So many years ago, and I still remember. One had a scar on his forehead and a broken nose. Another had no teeth. Today it is as terrible years ago. They beat me on the floor and I couldn't close my eyes when they caught hold of Leah. God will not forget. I will not let Him. Cancers are eating their flesh. They have murdered each other with guns. All, all, and the good foolish ones, too, their children deny them——

Shoo! Shoo!

Cossacks . . .!

Yes, in Russia, of course. A village, a small place. Two lines of wooden houses it had, like two short lines of upright writing, and a bad smell between the lines. The rabbi said: 'A Jew's house must be clean. Can clean people inhabit an unclean house? No more than a pure soul can dwell in a sinful body.' So what do they do, the clean Jews! All their dirt they threw out of their houses into the street—and it smelled. Lord! Lord! how it smelled!

Eh, sometimes when I'm lonely up here, and cold, I remember that smell. I remember when I was coming back from my first visit to Petersburg, how I noticed that smell. We weren't permitted to enter Petersburg without passports, and Jews weren't supposed to be living there; but permissions are for those that can't evade them, eh? Petersburg! What a town that was! Women with jewels thick on their flesh like rasp-berries on a bush in the summertime: great dukes and grand

dukes, princes and princesses, and business men with fur coats
—ach, in Petersburg everybody wore fur coats!—and stone
houses—such houses! better than Germany, better than great
England—palaces they were, I tell you! Miriam, my sister-in-
law, took me on a sleigh over a bridge to a place called Islands.
Was that a drive? A drive in the cold night under the white
moon, and the tinkle-tinkle of the tiny bells, and the pud-a-
pud-pud of the horses' hooves on the hard snow, and the wind
in our eyes, and the ice-flakes settling on our furs, and our
warm hands down under the cover like in a poem by Pushkin
I used to know, word for word by heart. I've forgotten it now.
Such a drive!

Ai, ai, the things an old cracked fellow remembers! My
mama used to say to me: 'Chaim, why do you sit so still? You
are too young for memories. . . .' Lucky One, Lucky One they
used to call me! I was so lucky. Whatever I touched was lucky
that day. Eh, see now, how things turn out! When I was little
enough to be carried the women used to take me with them
when they went for their holy bath. They wanted to see me
for luck when they came out. And hence am I the pioneer; I
have gone before. Oh, believe me, Fellows, it is as easy to
understand my journey to the moon as it is to believe that I
am locked up in a madhouse! Ponder this carefully. . . . It is
a necessary thing. . . . Only keep it to yourselves, do, keep it
secret.

Or else, woe betide us all. Heed my warning, hear my
prophecy. Our last refuge will shrink to a silly silver button
in the sky and there'll be only the world, only the wilderness
for us. And wild beasts shall tear at us and devour our
children. I prophesy! I prophesy! As before, till doomsday the
Jews will be running here and scurrying there like mice in a
barn. As before, outcasts from the nations, unhomed, nomadic
in a world of desert. As before, from Egypt, from Babylon,
from Rome, Spain, Russia, Germany . . . some will deny themselves, some will be resigned and wait for better times, some
will expect the Messiah, some will identify themselves with all
who do not worship idols and think they suffer for another

humanity, some will die without hope, some will be born without hope—none, none will be undisquieted. In those days men will not change. Men will be as they were before; in the shops, in the schools, in the places of sin, the homes and the places of worship: greedy, cunning, diseased, helpless, afraid; and the Jews too are men. But in the Ladder of Jacob is our salvation. I see, I see our people like a flight of swallows across the firmament, baffling astronomy, swifting to the moon. To the moon. What do you leave behind, fellows? A shambles, the cemetery of humanity!

Oh, my foolish eyes! my poor daft brain! What am I to speak prophecy? A weakwit Jew in a madhouse. In a lunatic asylum where you can't even get a drop to drink when your throat is like sand. Every other day the doctor comes to me. He tells me I am well, I can go. Where shall I go? I am a Jew. I have no place to go. As before, as always, this way or that way, back and forward, wanderers, wanderers. . . .

When the Reds came to our village, they said: 'Eh, dirty Jews, they are against the Revolution!' Cossacks came and said: 'Feh, dirty Jews, they are all revolutionaries!' After they had gone I dug the grave with my own hands and I buried Leah. I had no water to wash the bloodstains off her mouth. I threw earth on her, on Leah the practical woman, my wife. It was night, starless, and my mind was dark. I took Isaac, the little one, and ran in the night. I became a refugee. What sights, what sufferings! God be thanked, I had money, I escaped. I reached Hamburg.

Isaac said to me: 'Why do we run away from home? Why don't we stay and beat the bad men?' 'Hush,' I told him. 'There is a reason for all things.' True, and when I noticed the Man in the Moon thinking hard all the time I said to him: 'Mister, about what are you thinking?' 'I'm thinking', he said, 'why should there by a Y in God.' This puzzled me. 'Why should there be a Y in God?' Because there is no Y in God. 'Excuse me, mister,' I said, 'I'm thinking . . . but . . . why *should* there by a Y in God?' 'That's what I'm thinking,' said the Man in the Moon.

Yes, yes, ideas, ideas . . . In Germany at that time the people talked about nothing else except world brotherhood and socialism and the oppressed minorities. In Germany a Jew could breathe, he could lift up his head. In Nuremberg I had a cousin, and he took me into his business, in the toy trade, and Isaac went to school like a German boy. So it was. Every beginning has an end if we had sight to see it; but we go in the dark like bats and see little and soon forget what we have seen.

My cousin wanted an agent in England, so I went to England; and I came back to Nuremberg, and I went to England again. The years passed down like rain from the sky. . . . Ai, ai, for what are our eyes? I was too old for journeys. England was my home. I could get a game of chess, I could read a book, I could talk politics. I was satisfied! Always I told myself: 'Tomorrow. Tomorrow. Next day and next day I will go back to Germany to see my boy Isaac.' My boy? A man now. The last time I saw him he was a big handsome fellow of twenty-two. A student. A thinker. A dreamer! He joined the communists, and I used to argue with him. 'What use are the communists, ah? These are all ideas. When you are as old as I am you will understand. Can names change things? Communists, nihilists, anarchists—aren't they men? When they don't need the Jew they'll spit on him as soon as any Cossack!' But my boy used to get angry at me talking that way. 'It's a new generation, a new life,' he used to tell me. 'You don't understand.'

Well, I didn't understand. The young and the old speak different tongues, but they have the same meaning all the same. He often sent me money in his letters from Nuremberg. He had passed through the college there. He was a doctor now. Eh, how I used to talk of him! My boy this and my boy that— always my boy! Wonderful letters came from him every Monday morning. They made my heart glow. For what? To get parched black here in a madhouse. And when I die the Christians promise me their hell for a habitation. . . .

Pfui! Ach, it's cold up here. It nips the tip of the nose, it does, and the tips of the toes. It is an effort to keep alive . . .

my ten fingers are like ten icicles. But better here than wandering. Perhaps I am not so mad, after all. Who can tell? The doctor is an anti-semite and a fool. 'You can go tomorrow,' he says to me. Was there ever a Jew that was not pushed out from somewhere? He can't even stay in a madhouse. 'You can go tomorrow.' Where can I go? An anti-semite! *Shoo! Shoo!* Thank God for the moon. Here I am safe. No one can push me out of the moon. Hah! More of them? *Shoo! Shoo!* What a life for a man!

Fellow racials, you can travel all the continents of the world, and walk the streets of great cities, and creep into caves, but there is nowhere you can find peace except on the moon. I will tell you how to reach me if you have patience, but first you must hear about Isaac.

So one Monday morning there came a letter, and it said that my boy was going to be married. Money was in the letter too, for me to come over to the wedding. Also a photograph of a young woman. Ai, a beauty she was, I tell you. White like milk and plump as a pumpkin. Did my heart beat? Was I overjoyed? Ai, ai, what a bubble dream it was! I babbled like a crazy one. My son had bought a house in Nuremberg. The girl's family were making a big wedding in Berlin. I never knew how much the dowry was. Believe me, it was a good dowry. My boy was no fool.

So. Then they showed me the newspaper. Who lives now in the house in Nuremberg? A list of names I read in the newspaper showing how many Jews and Communists had been murdered in Germany. At first it might have been a mistake. Newspapers are written by men. It had my boy's name and his title and address, everything. I kept quiet. I waited. Then I don't know . . . a noise in my brain like a big clock before it strikes, lights, whispers, the sound of an iron door that swung and shut. Immediately I was mad. The doctor stood up and rubbed his chin. 'You are well now,' he said. 'You can go tomorrow.' When he had gone I sat on my bed and watched the ceiling. It had a crack thin as a hair on it, but I saw it. I sat and thought and watched the ceiling. 'Eh,' I said to myself, and I couldn't help chuckling. 'Eh, I'll do something about this. He thinks he can push me out. And if I go out I'll only have to find another madhouse. There are anti-semites everywhere. Then I'll be pushed out from the next place. And so on . . . No,' I said to myself, 'I'm old and tired and I'm sick of wandering.' And would you believe it, just as I said that, the crack in the ceiling began to swell! It widened and widened, and widened, and it began to open out like a great mouth yawning, and it went on opening and widening. Believe me, at first I was in a fright. I sat on my bed and I trembled. Such a thing to happen! Who ever heard of such a thing? I trembled, and I sweated, and I beat my breast. 'More trouble,' I said to myself. 'That's what it is. Ai! An unfortunate man I am. I can't sit on my bed but the ceiling must begin to open! Where is the sense in it, ah?'

Now, I ask you, what was I to do? I began to shiver all over. I was afraid to look up. For all I knew it might have been a trick on me by the doctor. How was I to tell that it was not a trick to get me out of the place? It was a delicate business, take it from me. Eh, so what did I do? I closed my eyes, I put my hands over my ears, and I just stayed there like that for a long time.

All of a sudden I knew it was not a trick. The doctor was not such a fool to go and break up a good ceiling. I opened my eyes and I jumped up, quick as an acrobat, through the crack. Up I soared, up, up, like a bird, into the sky. The whole day I kept on going up and up and up, and the Sabbath star was just coming out when I passed it. It winked at me, and I nodded my head. Then my head pushed up among a mess of stars like a diver in the water coming up among seaweed. I went on up all glistening from the stars. Soon I felt coldness on my forehead and I straightened myself and stepped out on the moon. But imagine my surprise when the Man in the Moon ran up to me and began shaking my hand and said hallo to me in Yiddish. '*Sholem aleichem*,' he said. '*Aleichem sholem*,' said I. 'Well,' he said, 'how's business?' 'Business?' I said. 'What sort of business can you do in a madhouse?' 'Well,' he said, 'if you can't do business in a madhouse, tell me, how do you expect to do business on the moon?' 'Expect?' I said. 'Who expects? I expect nothing! I just came to have a look round.' 'A *look*?' he said. 'You can *look* as much as you like!'

My word, fellows, it's a paradise! To think it was up there in the sky all the time and nobody thought of it. The perfectest dwelling-place. And when the Man in the Moon and I became friends and I said to him: 'This is the way it is. The Jews are thrown out of this country and out of that country all over the world . . .'; so he said to me: 'If that is the case, why don't they come and live up here, eh?'

I talk! I talk! No one comes to put on the light. I am as thirsty as the Palestinian sands. What sorrow, too, knocks at my heart! No one comes. The moonlight has gone out. The world is altogether dark. I tell you, I have staked claims for all of us on the moon, but they don't treat me well in this place. I am an old fellow, and I dislike the other people here. In fact, I honestly think that the whole pack of them are mad. . . . It's about time I was dead. In the grave you don't feel cold, you don't feel thirsty, you don't feel anything. And there are so many children in the world after all. . . . What does an old man matter? Ai, ai! Better under the earth.